VIRAGO
MODERN CLASSICS

Virago was founded in 1973 in association with Quartet, and became a fully independent company three years later, publishing this, its first book, *Life as We Have Known It* by Co-operative Working Women in 1977. This book launched the new Virago and The Virago Reprint Library which later included *Maternity* (now republished as *No One But a Woman Knows*). Inspired by, among other things, Sheila Rowbotham's *Hidden from History*, the Virago Reprint Library fed an eager new audience's de~~~~~

THE CO-OPERATIVE

Today, the Co-operative Women's Guild is much smaller than it used to be, with both fewer branches and members; however, its aims and objectives remain the same as when it first started in 1883.

The guild remains committed to the Co-operative Movement and to helping local communities. It fundraises for chosen local and national charities and campaigns on causes that affect many people, such as recent changes to the NHS.

Lyn Longbottom
National President, 2011–12

LIFE AS WE HAVE KNOWN IT

The Voices of Working-Class Women

Edited by Margaret Llewelyn Davies

virago

VIRAGO

First published by Virago Press Limited in 1977
This edition published by Virago Press in 2012

First published in Great Britain by the Hogarth Press Limited in 1931
Introductory Letter by Virginia Woolf

Introduction copyright © Anna Davin and Gloden Dallas 1977

The moral right of the author has been asserted

A CIP catalogue record for this book
is available from the British Library.

ISBN 978-1-84408-801-0

Typeset in Goudy by M Rules
Printed and bound in Great Britain by
Clays Ltd, St Ives plc

Papers used by Virago are from well-managed forests
and other responsible sources.

MIX
Paper from
responsible sources
FSC® C104740

Virago Press
An imprint of
Little, Brown Book Group
100 Victoria Embankment
London EC4Y 0DY

An Hachette UK Company
www.hachette.co.uk

www.virago.co.uk

LIFE AS WE
HAVE KNOWN IT

The Voices of
Working-Class Women

CONTENTS

Introductory Letter To Margaret Llewelyn Davies

By Virginia Woolf

When you asked me to write a preface to a book which you had collected of papers by working women I replied that I would be drowned rather than write a preface to any book whatsoever. Books should stand on their own feet, my argument was (and I think it is a sound one). If they need shoring up by a preface here, an introduction there, they have no more right to exist than a table that needs a wad of paper under one leg in order to stand steady. But you left me the papers, and, turning them over, I saw that on this occasion the argument did not apply; this book is not a book. Turning the pages, I began to ask myself what is this book then, if it is not a book? What quality has it? What ideas does it suggest? What old arguments and memories does it rouse in me? And as all this had nothing to do with an introduction or a preface, but brought you to mind and certain pictures from the past, I stretched my hand for a sheet of notepaper and wrote the following letter addressed not to the public but to you.

You have forgotten (I wrote) a hot June morning in Newcastle in the year 1913, or at least you will not remember what I remember, because you were otherwise engaged. Your attention was entirely absorbed by a green table, several sheets of paper, and a bell. Moreover you were frequently interrupted. There was a woman wearing something like a Lord Mayor's chain round her shoulders; she took her seat perhaps at your right; there were other women without ornament save fountain pens and despatch boxes – they sat perhaps at your left. Soon a row had been formed up there on the platform, with tables and inkstands and tumblers of water; while we, many hundreds of us, scraped and shuffled and filled the entire body of some vast municipal building beneath. The proceedings somehow opened. Perhaps an organ played. Perhaps songs were sung. Then the talking and the laughing suddenly subsided. A bell struck; a figure rose; a woman took her way from among us; she mounted a platform; she spoke for precisely five minutes; she descended. Directly she sat down another woman rose; mounted the platform; spoke for precisely five minutes and descended; then a third rose, then a fourth – and so it went on, speaker following speaker, one from the right, one from the left, one from the middle, one from the background – each took her way to the stand, said what she had to say, and gave place to her successor. There was something military in the regularity of the proceeding. They were like marksmen, I thought, standing up in turn with rifle raised to aim at a target. Sometimes they missed, and there was a roar of laughter; sometimes they hit, and there was a roar of applause. But whether the particular shot hit or missed there was no doubt about the carefulness of the aim. There was no beating the bush; there were no phrases of easy eloquence. The speaker made her way to the stand primed with her subject. Determination and resolution were stamped on her face. There was so much to be said between the strokes of the bell that she could not waste one second. The moment had come for which she had been waiting, perhaps for many months. The moment had come for which she had stored hat, shoes and dress – there was an air of discreet novelty about her clothing. But above all the moment had come when she was going to speak her mind, the mind of her constituency, the mind of the women who had sent her from Devonshire, perhaps, or Sussex, or some black mining village in Yorkshire to speak their mind for them in Newcastle.

It soon became obvious that the mind which lay spread over so wide a stretch of England was a vigorous mind working with great activity. It was thinking in June 1913 of the reform of the Divorce Laws; of the taxation of land values; of the Minimum Wage. It was concerned with the care of maternity; with the Trades Board Act; with the education of children over fourteen; it was unanimously of opinion that Adult Suffrage should become a Government measure – it was thinking in short about every sort of public question, and it was thinking constructively and pugnaciously. Accrington did not see eye to eye with Halifax, nor Middlesbrough with Plymouth. There was argument and opposition; resolutions were lost and amendments won. Hands shot up stiff as swords, or were pressed as stiffly to the side. Speaker followed speaker; the morning was cut up into precise lengths of five minutes by the bell.

Meanwhile – let me try after seventeen years to sum up the thoughts that passed through the minds of your guests, who had come from London and elsewhere, not to take part, but to listen – meanwhile what was it all about?

What was the meaning of it? These women were demanding divorce, education, the vote – all good things. They were demanding higher wages and shorter hours – what could be more reasonable? And yet, though it was all so reasonable, much of it so forcible, some of it so humorous, a weight of discomfort was settling and shifting itself uneasily from side to side in your visitors' minds. All these questions – perhaps this was at the bottom of it – which matter so intensely to the people here, questions of sanitation and education and wages, this demand for an extra shilling, for another year at school, for eight hours instead of nine behind a counter or in a mill, leave me, in my own blood and bones, untouched. If every reform they demand was granted this very instant it would not touch one hair of my comfortable capitalistic head. Hence my interest is merely altruistic. It is thin spread and moon coloured. There is no life blood or urgency about it. However hard I clap my hands or stamp my feet there is a hollowness in the sound which betrays me. I am a benevolent spectator. I am irretrievably cut off from the actors. I sit here hypocritically clapping and stamping, an outcast from the flock. On top of this too, my reason (it was in 1913, remember) could not help assuring me that even if the resolution, whatever it was, were carried unanimously the stamping and the clapping was an empty noise. It would pass out of the open window and become part of the clamour of the lorries and the striving of the hooves on the cobbles of Newcastle beneath – an inarticulate uproar. The mind might be active; the mind might be aggressive; but the mind was without a body; it had no legs or arms with which to enforce its will. In all that audience, among all those women who worked, who bore children, who scrubbed and cooked and bargained, there was not a single woman with a vote. Let them fire off their rifles if they liked, but they would hit no target; there were only blank cartridges inside. The thought was irritating and depressing in the extreme.

The clock had now struck half-past eleven. Thus there were still then many hours to come. And if one had reached this stage of irritation and depression by half-past eleven in the morning, into what depths of boredom and despair would one not be plunged by half-past five in the evening? How could one sit out another day of speechifying? How could one, above all, face you, our hostess, with the information that your Congress had proved so insupportably exacerbating that one was going back to London by the very first train? The only chance lay in some happy conjuring trick, some change of attitude by which the mist and blankness of the speeches could be turned to blood and bone. Otherwise they remained intolerable. But suppose one played a childish game; suppose one said, as a child says, 'Let's pretend.' 'Let's pretend,' one said to oneself, looking at the speaker, 'that I am Mrs Giles of Durham City.' A woman of that name had just turned to address us. 'I am the wife of a miner. He comes back thick with grime. First he must have his bath. Then he must have his supper. But there is only a copper. My range is crowded with saucepans. There is no getting on with the work. All my crocks are covered with dust again. Why in the Lord's name have I not hot water and electric light laid on when middle-class women ...' So up I jump and demand passionately 'labour saving appliances and housing reform.' Up I jump in the person of Mrs Giles of Durham; in the person of Mrs Phillips of Bacup; in the person of Mrs Edwards of Wolverton. But after all the imagination is largely the child of the flesh. One could not be Mrs Giles of Durham because one's body had never stood at the wash-tub; one's hands had never wrung and scrubbed and chopped up whatever the meat may be that makes a miner's supper. The picture therefore was always letting in irrelevancies. One sat in an armchair

or read a book. One saw landscapes and seascapes, perhaps Greece or Italy, where Mrs Giles or Mrs Edwards
must have seen slag heaps and rows upon rows of slate-
roofed houses. Something was always creeping in from
a world that was not their world and making the picture false and the game too much of a game to be worth
playing.

It was true that one could always correct these fancy
portraits by taking a look at the actual person – at Mrs
Thomas, or Mrs Langrish, or Miss Bolt of Hebden Bridge.
They were worth looking at. Certainly, there were no
armchairs, or electric light, or hot water laid on in their
lives; no Greek hills or Mediterranean bays in their
dreams. Bakers and butchers did not call for orders. They
did not sign a cheque to pay the weekly bills, or order,
over the telephone, a cheap but quite adequate seat at the
Opera. If they travelled it was on excursion day, with food
in string bags and babies in their arms. They did not stroll
through the house and say, that cover must go to the
wash, or those sheets need changing. They plunged their
arms in hot water and scrubbed the clothes themselves.
In consequence their bodies were thick-set and muscular,
their hands were large, and they had the slow emphatic
gestures of people who are often stiff and fall tired in a

heap on hard-backed chairs. They touched nothing lightly. They gripped papers and pencils as if they were brooms. Their faces were firm and heavily folded and lined with deep lines. It seemed as if their muscles were always taut and on the stretch. Their eyes looked as if they were always set on something actual – on saucepans that were boiling over, on children who were getting into mischief. Their lips never expressed the lighter and more detached emotions that come into play when the mind is perfectly at ease about the present. No, they were not in the least detached and easy and cosmopolitan. They were indigenous and rooted to one spot. Their very names were like the stones of the fields – common, grey, worn, obscure, docked of all splendours of association and romance. Of course they wanted baths and ovens and education and seventeen shillings instead of sixteen, and freedom and air and ... 'And,' said Mrs Winthrop of Spennymoor, breaking into these thoughts with words that sounded like a refrain, 'we can wait.' ... 'Yes,' she repeated, as if she had waited so long that the last lap of that immense vigil meant nothing for the end was in sight, 'we can wait.' And she got down rather stiffly from her perch and made her way back to her seat, an elderly woman dressed in her best clothes.

Then Mrs Potter spoke. Then Mrs Elphick. Then Mrs Holmes of Edgbaston. So it went on, and at last after innumerable speeches, after many communal meals at long tables and many arguments – the world was to be reformed, from top to bottom, in a variety of ways – after seeing Co-operative jams bottled and Co-operative biscuits made, after some song singing and ceremonies with banners, the new President received the chain of office with a kiss from the old President; the Congress dispersed; and the separate members who had stood up so valiantly and spoken out so boldly while the clock ticked its five minutes went back to Yorkshire and Wales and Sussex and Devonshire, and hung their clothes in the wardrobe and plunged their hands in the wash-tub again.

Later that summer the thoughts here so inadequately described, were again discussed, but not in a public hall hung with banners and loud with voices. The head office of the Guild, the centre from which speakers, papers, inkstands and tumblers, as I suppose, issued, was then in Hampstead. There, if I may remind you again of what you may well have forgotten, you invited us to come; you asked us to tell you how the Congress had impressed us. But I must pause on the threshold of that very dignified old house, with its eighteenth-century carvings and panelling, as we paused then in truth, for one could not enter and go upstairs without encountering Miss Kidd. Miss Kidd sat at her typewriter in the outer office. Miss Kidd, one felt, had set herself as a kind of watch-dog to ward off the meddlesome middle-class wasters of time who come prying into other people's business. Whether it was for this reason that she was dressed in a peculiar shade of deep purple I do not know. The colour seemed somehow symbolical. She was very short, but, owing to the weight which sat on her brow and the gloom which seemed to issue from her dress, she was also very heavy. An extra share of the world's grievances seemed to press upon her shoulders. When she clicked her typewriter one felt that she was making that instru-ment transmit messages of foreboding and ill-omen to an unheeding universe. But she relented, and like all relentings after gloom her's came with a sudden charm. Then we went upstairs, and upstairs we came upon a very different figure – upon Miss Lilian Harris, indeed, who, whether it was due to her dress which was coffee coloured, or to her smile which was serene, or to the ash-tray in which many cigarettes had come amiably to an end, seemed the image of detachment and equanim-ity. Had one not known that Miss Harris was to the

Congress what the heart is to the remoter veins – that the great engine at Newcastle would not have thumped and throbbed without her – that she had collected and sorted and summoned and arranged that very intricate but orderly assembly of women – she would never have enlightened one. She had nothing whatever to do; she licked a few stamps and addressed a few envelopes – it was a fad of hers – that was what her manner conveyed. It was Miss Harris who moved the papers off the chairs and got the tea-cups out of the cupboard. It was she who answered questions about figures and put her hand on the right file of letters infallibly and sat listening, without saying very much, but with calm comprehension, to whatever was said.

Again let me telescope into a few sentences, and into one scene many random discussions on various occasions at various places. We said then – for you now emerged from an inner room, and if Miss Kidd was purple and Miss Harris was coffee coloured, you, speaking pictorially (and I dare not speak more explicitly) were kingfisher blue and as arrowy and decisive as that quick bird – we said then that the Congress had roused thoughts and ideas of the most diverse nature. It had been a revelation and a disillusionment. We had been humiliated and enraged. To begin with, all their talk, we said, or the greater part of it, was of matters of fact. They want baths and money. To expect us, whose minds, such as they are, fly free at the end of a short length of capital to tie ourselves down again to that narrow plot of acquisitiveness and desire is impossible. We have baths and we have money. Therefore, however much we had sympathised our sympathy was largely fictitious. It was aesthetic sympathy, the sympathy of the eye and of the imagination, not of the heart and of the nerves; and such sympathy is always physically uncomfortable. Let us explain what we mean, we said. The Guild's women are magnificent to look at. Ladies in evening dress are lovelier far, but they lack the sculpturesque quality that these working women have. And though the range of expression is narrower in working women, their few expressions have a force and an emphasis, of tragedy or humour, which the faces of ladies lack. But, at the same time, it is much better to be a lady; ladies desire Mozart and Einstein – that is, they desire things that are ends, not things that are means. Therefore to deride ladies and to imitate, as some of the speakers did, their mincing speech and little knowledge of what it pleases them to call 'reality' is, so it seems to us, not merely foolish but gives away the whole purpose of the

Congress, for if it is better to be working women by all means let them remain so and not undergo the contamination which wealth and comfort bring. In spite of this, we went on, apart from prejudice and bandying compliments, undoubtedly the women at the Congress possess something which ladies lack, and something which is desirable, which is stimulating, and yet very difficult to define. One does not want to slip easily into fine phrases about 'contact with life,' about 'facing facts' and 'the teaching of experience,' for they invariably alienate the hearer, and moreover no working man or woman works harder or is in closer touch with reality than a painter with his brush or a writer with his pen. But the quality that they have, judging from a phrase caught here and there, from a laugh, or a gesture seen in passing, is precisely the quality that Shakespeare would have enjoyed. One can fancy him slipping away from the brilliant salons of educated people to crack a joke in Mrs Robson's back kitchen. Indeed, we said, one of our most curious impressions at your Congress was that the 'poor,' 'the working classes,' or by whatever name you choose to call them, are not downtrodden, envious and exhausted; they are humorous and vigorous and thoroughly independent. Thus if it were possible to meet them not as masters or mistresses or customers with a counter between us, but over the wash-tub or in the parlour casually and congenially as fellow-beings with the same wishes and ends in view, a great liberation would follow, and perhaps friendship and sympathy would supervene. How many words must lurk in those women's vocabularies that have faded from ours! How many scenes must lie dormant in their eye which are unseen by ours! What images and saws and proverbial sayings must still be current with them that have never reached the surface of print, and very likely they still keep the power which we have lost of making new ones. There were many shrewd sayings in the speeches at Congress which even the weight of a public meeting could not flatten out entirely. But, we said, and here perhaps fiddled with a paper knife, or poked the fire impatiently by way of expressing our discontent, what is the use of it all? Our sympathy is fictitious, not real. Because the baker calls and we pay our bills with cheques, and our clothes are washed for us and we do not know the liver from the lights, we are condemned to remain forever shut up in the confines of the middle classes, wearing tail coats and silk stockings, and called Sir or Madam as the case may be, when we are all, in truth, simply Johns and Susans. And they remain equally deprived. For we have

as much to give them as they to give us – wit and detachment, learning and poetry, and all those good gifts
which those who have never answered bells or minded
machines enjoy by right. But the barrier is impassable.
And nothing perhaps exacerbated us more at the Congress
(you must have noticed at times a certain irritability)
than the thought that this force of theirs, this smoulder-
ing heat which broke the crust now and then and licked
the surface with a hot and fearless flame, is about to
break through and melt us together so that life will be
richer and books more complex and society will pool its
possessions instead of segregating them – all this is going
to happen inevitably, thanks to you, very largely, and to
Miss Harris and to Miss Kidd – but only when we are
dead.

It was thus that we tried in the Guild Office that afternoon to explain the nature of fictitious sympathy and
how it differs from real sympathy and how defective it is
because it is not based upon sharing the same important
emotions unconsciously. It was thus that we tried to
describe the contradictory and complex feelings which
beset the middle-class visitor when forced to sit out a
Congress of working women in silence.

Perhaps it was at this point that you unlocked a drawer

and took out a packet of papers. You did not at once untie the string that fastened them. Sometimes, you said, you got a letter which you could not bring yourself to burn; once or twice a Guildswoman had at your suggestion written a few pages about her life. It might be that we should find these papers interesting; that if we read them the women would cease to be symbols and would become instead individuals. But they were very fragmentary and ungrammatical; they had been jotted down in the intervals of housework. Indeed you could not at once bring yourself to give them up, as if to expose them to other eyes were a breach of confidence. It might be that their crudity would only perplex, that the writing of people who do not know how to write – but at this point we burst in. In the first place, every Englishwoman knows how to write; in the second, even if she does not she has only to take her own life for subject and write the truth about that and not fiction or poetry for our interest to be so keenly roused that – that in short we cannot wait but must read the packet at once.

Thus pressed you did by degrees and with many delays – there was the war for example, and Miss Kidd died, and you and Lilian Harris retired from the Guild, and a testimonial was given you in a casket, and many thousands of working women tried to say how you had changed their lives – tried to say what they will feel for you to their dying day – after all these interruptions you did at last gather the papers together and finally put them in my hands early this May. There they were, typed and docketed with a few snapshots and rather faded photographs stuck between the pages. And when at last I began to read, there started up in my mind's eye the figures that I had seen all those years ago at Newcastle with such bewilderment and curiosity. But they were no longer addressing a large meeting in Newcastle from a platform, dressed in their best clothes. The hot June day with its banners and its ceremonies had vanished, and instead one looked back into the past of the women who had stood there; into the four-roomed houses of miners, into the homes of small shopkeepers and agricultural labourers, into the fields and factories of fifty or sixty years ago. Mrs Burrows, for example, had worked in the Lincolnshire fens when she was eight with forty or fifty other children, and an old man had followed the gang with a long whip in his hand 'which he did not forget to use.' That was a strange reflection. Most of the women had started work at seven or eight, earning a penny on Saturday for washing a doorstep, or twopence a week for carrying suppers to the men at the iron foundry. They had gone into factories when they were fourteen. They had worked from seven in the morning till eight or nine at night and had made thirteen or fifteen shillings a week. Out of this money they had saved some pence with which to buy their mother gin – she was often very tired in the evening and had borne perhaps thirteen children in as many years; or they fetched opium to assuage some miserable old woman's ague in the fens. Old Betty Rollett killed herself when she could get no more. They had seen half-starved women standing in rows to be paid for their match-boxes while they snuffed the roast meat of their employer's dinner cooking within. The smallpox had raged in Bethnal Green and they had known that the boxes went on being made in the sick-room and were sold to the public with the infection still thick on them. They had been so cold working in the wintry fields that they could not run when the ganger gave them leave. They had waded through floods when the Wash over-flowed its banks. Kind old ladies had given them parcels of food which had turned out to contain only crusts of bread and rancid bacon rind. All this they had done and seen and known when other children were still dabbling in seaside pools and spelling out fairy tales by the nursery fire. Naturally their faces had a different look on them. But they were, one remembered, firm faces, faces with something indomitable in their expression. Astonishing though it seems, human nature is so tough that it will take such wounds, even at the tenderest age, and survive them. Keep a child mewed in Bethnal Green and she will somehow snuff the country air from seeing the yellow dust on her brother's boots, and nothing will serve her but she must go there and see the 'clean ground,' as she calls it, for herself. It was true that at first the 'bees were very frightening,' but all the same she got to the country and the blue smoke and the cows came up to her expectation. Put girls, after a childhood of minding smaller brothers and washing doorsteps, into a factory when they are fourteen and their eyes will turn to the window and they will be happy because, as the workroom is six storeys high, the sun can be seen breaking over the hills, 'and that was always such a comfort and help.' Still stranger, if one needs additional proof of the strength of the human instinct to escape from bondage and attach itself whether to a country road or to a sunrise over the hills, is the fact that the highest ideals of duty flourish in an obscure hat factory as surely as on a battlefield. There were women in Christies' felt hat factory, for example, who worked for 'honour.' They gave their lives to the cause of putting straight stitches into the bindings of men's hat brims. Felt is hard and thick; it is difficult to push the needle through; there are no rewards or glory to be won; but such is the incorrigible idealism of the human mind that there were 'trimmers' in those obscure places who would never put a crooked stitch in their work and ruthlessly tore out the crooked stitches of others. And as they drove in their straight stitches they reverenced Queen Victoria and thanked God, drawing up to the fire, that they were all married to good Conservative working men.

Certainly that story explained something of the force, of the obstinacy, which one had seen in the faces of the speakers at Newcastle. And then, if one went on reading these papers, one came upon other signs of the extraordinary vitality of the human spirit. That inborn energy which no amount of childbirth and washing up can quench had reached out, it seemed, and seized upon old copies of magazines; had attached itself to Dickens; had propped the poems of Burns against a dish cover to read while cooking. They read at meals; they read before going to the mill. They read Dickens and Scott and Henry George and Bulwer Lytton and Ella Wheeler Wilcox and Alice Meynell and would like 'to get hold of any good history of the French Revolution, not Carlyle's, please,' and B. Russell on China, and William Morris and Shelley and Florence Barclay and Samuel Butler's Note Books – they read with the indiscriminate greed of a hungry appetite, that crams itself with toffee and beef and tarts and vinegar and champagne all in one gulp. Naturally such reading led to argument. The younger generation had the audacity to say that Queen Victoria was no better than an honest charwoman who had brought up her children respectably. They had the temerity to doubt whether to sew straight stitches into men's hat brims should be the sole aim and end of a woman's life. They started arguments and even held rudimentary debating societies on the floor of the factory. In time the old trimmers even were shaken in their beliefs and came to think that there might be other ideals in the world besides straight stitches and Queen Victoria. Strange ideas indeed were seething in their brain. A girl, for instance, would reason, as she walked along the streets of a factory town, that she had no right to bring a child into the world if that child must earn its living in a mill. A chance saying in a book would fire her imagination to dream of future cities where there were to be baths and kitchens and washhouses and art galleries and museums and parks. The minds of working women were humming and their imaginations were awake. But how were they to realise their ideals? How were they to express their needs? It was hard enough for middle class women with some amount of money and some degree of education behind them. But how could women whose hands were full of work, whose kitchens were thick with steam, who had neither education nor encouragement nor leisure remodel the world according to the ideas of working women? It was then, I suppose, sometime in the eighties, that the Women's Guild crept modestly and tentatively into existence. For a time it occupied an inch or two of space in the *Co-operative News* which called itself The Women's Corner. It was there that Mrs Acland asked, 'Why should we not hold our Co-operative mothers' meetings, when we may bring our work and sit together, one of us reading some Co-operative work aloud, which may afterwards be discussed?' And on April 18th, 1883, she announced that the Women's Guild now numbered seven members. It was the Guild then that drew to itself all that restless wishing and dreaming. It was the Guild that made a central meeting place where formed and solidified all that was else so scattered and incoherent. The Guild must have given the older women, with their husbands and children, what 'clean ground' had given to the little girl in Bethnal Green, or the view of day breaking over the hills had given the girls in the hat factory. It gave them in the first place the rarest of all possessions – a room where they could sit down and think remote from boiling saucepans and crying children; and then that room became not merely a sitting-room and a meeting place, but a workshop where, laying their heads together, they could remodel their houses, could remodel their lives, could beat out this reform and that. And, as the membership grew, and twenty or thirty women made a practice of meeting weekly, so their ideas increased, and their interests widened. Instead of discussing merely their own taps and their own sinks and their own long hours and little pay, they began to discuss education and taxation and the conditions of work in the country at large. The women who had crept modestly in 1883 into Mrs Acland's sitting-room to sew and 'read some Co-operative work aloud,' learnt to speak out, boldly and authoritatively, about every question of civic life. Thus it came about that Mrs Robson and Mrs Potter and Mrs Wright at Newcastle in 1913 were asking not only for baths and wages and electric light, but also for adult suffrage and the taxation of land values and divorce law reform. Thus in a year or two they were to demand peace and disarmament and the spread of Co-operative principles, not only among the working people of Great Britain, but among the nations of the world. And the force that lay behind their speeches and drove them home beyond the reach of eloquence was compact of many things – of men with whips, of sick rooms where match-boxes were made, of hunger and cold, of many and difficult childbirths, of much scrubbing and washing up, of reading Shelley and William Morris and Samuel Butler over the kitchen table, of weekly meetings of the Women's Guild, of Committees and Congresses at Manchester and elsewhere. All this lay behind the speeches of Mrs Robson and Mrs Potter and Mrs Wright. The papers which you sent me certainly threw some light upon the old curiosities and bewilderments which had made that Congress so memorable, and so thick with unanswered questions.

But that the pages here printed should mean all this to those who cannot supplement the written word with the memory of faces and the sound of voices is perhaps unlikely. It cannot be denied that the chapters here put together do not make a book – that as literature they have many limitations. The writing, a literary critic might say, lacks detachment and imaginative breadth, even as the women themselves lacked variety and play of feature. Here are no reflections, he might object, no view of life as a whole, and no attempt to enter into the lives of other people. Poetry and fiction seem far beyond their horizon. Indeed, we are reminded of those obscure writers before the birth of Shakespeare who never travelled beyond the borders of their own parishes, who read no language but their own, and wrote with difficulty, finding few words and those awkwardly. And yet since writing is a complex art, much infected by life, these pages have some qualities even as literature that the literate and instructed might envy. Listen, for instance, to Mrs Scott, the felt hat worker: 'I have been over the hilltops when the snow drifts were over three feet high, and six feet in some places. I was in a blizzard in Hayfield and thought I should never get round the corners. But it was life on the moors; I seemed to know every blade of grass and where the flowers grew and all the little streams were my companions.' Could she have said that better if Oxford had made her a Doctor of Letters? Or take Mrs Layton's description of a matchbox factory in Bethnal Green and how she looked through the fence and saw three ladies 'sitting in the shade doing some kind of fancy work.' It has something of the accuracy and clarity of a description by Defoe. And when Mrs Burrows brings to mind that bitter day when the children were about to eat their cold dinner and drink their cold tea under the hedge and the ugly woman asked them into her parlour saying, 'Bring these children into my house and let them eat their dinner there,' the words are simple, but it is difficult to see how they could say more. And then there is a fragment of a letter from Miss Kidd – the sombre purple figure who typed as if the weight of the world were on her shoulders. 'When I was a girl of seventeen,' she writes, 'my then employer, a gentleman of good position and high standing in the town, sent me to his home one night, ostensibly to take a parcel of books, but really with a very different object. When I arrived at the house all the family were away, and before he would allow me to leave he forced me to yield to him. At eighteen I was a mother.' Whether that is literature or not literature I do not presume to say, but that it explains much and reveals much is certain. Such then was the burden that rested on that sombre figure as she sat typing your letters, such were the memories she brooded as she guarded your door with her grim and indomitable fidelity.

But I will quote no more. These pages are only fragments. These voices are beginning only now to emerge from silence into half articulate speech. These lives are still half hidden in profound obscurity. To express even what is expressed here has been a work of labour and difficulty. The writing has been done in kitchens, at odds and ends of leisure, in the midst of distractions and obstacles – but really there is no need for me, in a letter addressed to you, to lay stress upon the hardship of working women's lives. Have not you and Lilian Harris given your best years – but hush! you will not let me finish that sentence and therefore, with the old messages of friendship and admiration, I will make an end.

May 1930.

Memories of Seventy Years

By Mrs Layton

1. Childhood in Bethnal Green.

I was born in Bethnal Green, April 9th, 1855, a tiny scrap of humanity. I was my mother's seventh child, and seven more were born after me – fourteen in all – which made my mother a perfect slave. Generally speaking, she was either expecting a baby to be born or had one at the breast. At the time there were eight of us the oldest was not big enough to get ready to go to school without help.

The house we lived in was a detached 'villa' in the parish of Bethnal Green, then a suburb of London, comprising three rooms on one floor, one room on each side of the front door, and a kitchen at the back which was so dark that it was only used on Saturdays, when the other room, which was the living room and children's bedroom, had a good clean and was made ready for Sunday. This house was built by my father and grandfather in their spare time for my mother to be brought to as a bride. It was surrounded by a very large garden, in fact every house in that part of Bethnal Green had a large garden, and nearly everyone kept either pigs or chickens or ducks – sometimes all three. The ground was the property of the Ecclesiastical Commissioners and let on short leases. There was no Local Authority to interfere with the methods adopted by the various builders, and each owner put up his house to suit his individual taste or convenience. Some preferred the house to stand close to the road with the garden behind. Others liked their house to stand right away from the road and the garden to be in front. The result was very undesirable, for it happened to many tenants, as it did to my parents, that their neighbours built their pigstyes at the end of the garden away from their own house, but close against the neighbour who had built his house in the opposite direction.

When I was about six years old, the lease of the house fell in, and we had to move to another part of the same parish, a thickly populated district where the people earned their living by book-making, wood-chopping and matchbox-making. The house contained two more rooms, but had only a small back-yard. I was fond of flowers and as there was no room in the back-yard to grow them, I grew them on my mother's bedroom windowsill, spending my halfpence in buying plants. It was the pride of my life when people admired them and began growing flowers too, and then our street did begin to look gay. At the back of the house a cowkeeper and dairyman kept in large sheds about forty milk cows. But very few people were able to buy milk in any quantity. In my own home milk was only used for tea when company came. The cows were turned out every day into a large yard which was only divided from our premises by a low wall. The smell was at times intolerable, and the flies in the summer were a perfect plague. Sanitation was never considered. The water-butt was placed outside the closet, which had no flush of water and smelt abominably. The ashes and house refuse were put in one corner of the yard only a few yards from the water-butt. This applied to all the other houses in the neighbourhood. As a result of the bad sanitation, epidemics of various kinds of fevers and of smallpox continually broke out. On one occasion cholera was so bad that many hundreds died.

Everyone had a lot of children. Some were too poor to let the children out to play because they had not enough clothes to cover them. On one occasion the children of one mother were left alone and they got out into the street with only a piece of sacking tied round them. They did look poor miserable little things, and the people who saw them began to look around to see if they had got something from their own scanty store that they could part with for their less fortunate neighbour.

My eldest sister, who has been all through my life one of my best friends, went into service at the age of twelve years old and always did well. When I was eight years old she was nurse to twin boys, whose smart clothes and fine perambulator set me longing to be a children's nurse when I grew up, and it was the delight of my life when one day some of the fine clothes cast off by the twins descended to my little brother. I shall never forget how well he looked in a pretty blue pelisse and cape, and I thought he was ever so much nicer looking than the previous wearer. I *was* proud of my little brother and I *did* wish he could always have nice clothes.

My fourth sister and I always stayed away from school on washing day to mind the babies. In the summer it was real sport, because so many people did their washing on the same day, and everybody had large families and generally kept the elder girls, and sometimes boys, at home to mind the little ones. We used to plan to go out all

4

together with our babies and prams into Victoria Park. Very few people had prams of their own, but could hire them at 1d. an hour to hold one baby, or 1½d. an hour to hold two. Several mothers would pay a few pence for the hire of a pram and the children used to manage between them how they were to be used. I need hardly say each pram was used to its full seating capacity. The single pram had always to accommodate two and the double pram three or more, and we always kept them the full length of time for which we had paid. We would picnic on bread and treacle under the trees in the Park, and return home in the evening a troop of tired but happy children.

I was rather a lazy little girl and not fond of washing myself. I am afraid I often went out in the morning without washing my face. One day when I was alone with my little brother in Victoria Park, a lady spoke to me and asked my age and if I went to school and a lot of other questions. She said I was a bright, intelligent little girl, and asked if I could read a few verses out of a nice Testament she had in her hand. I read the verses she pointed out – I don't remember what they were – but she said she was pleased I could read so nicely and advised me never to miss an opportunity of improving myself. Then she asked me if I had washed myself before I came out that morning. I felt so ashamed when I had to admit that I had not done so. Then she gave me the nice little Testament I had read from, and made me promise that I would never neglect to wash myself before leaving home either for school or play, and never to miss an opportunity of improving myself if only I had more time to give to educating myself.

The lure of the open country was almost as strong in my sister as in me, and one day we decided to walk to Epping Forest. So the first opportunity that presented itself we went, and carried our baby brother between us to Woodford. We had no idea of the distance, but we had made up our minds to go, and go we did. It took us all day to get there and back. My mother did not know of our intention, and it was only when the time came for my father to come home that she really got upset at our prolonged absence. Some of the children we played with told her where we were gone, and my father came as far as Hackney Church to meet us. When we saw him we expected a good thrashing, as we knew quite well we had no right to have stayed out all day. But we were surprised to see a relieved look come over his face and to hear him say he was glad to have found us and that we must be hungry. He took us into the only place that was open, a public house, and bought some bread and cheese for us, and carried baby home.

My father, a well-educated man, was employed in a government situation, working from 10 a.m. to 4 p.m. He was always steady and industrious, was a fine singer and very musical. He played in one of the bands of the old East India Company and was very proud of the fact that he played at the coronation of Queen Victoria. My father's position compelled him to keep up an appearance which an ordinary workman, earning the same wages, would not have had to do. He always went to business in nice black clothes and a silk hat. His appearance was quite out of keeping with the neighbourhood we lived in, and when he and my eldest brother came home in the evening I do not think people quite knew what to make of them. In his spare time he learnt the trade of a tailor and was able to augment his small salary by doing work for people who knew him and by growing nearly all the vegetables the family consumed. He was a churchman who never missed the Sunday morning service, and he always relieved my mother by taking several of the children with him. In politics he was a Conservative, but was always tolerant. A good father and husband up to a point, he left the responsibility of the whole family to my mother. She it was who had to start us all out in life.

As our family increased and my father's wages remained stationary, it was necessary for my mother to earn money to help to keep us in food and clothing. The clergyman's wife was very fond of her, and always had her to nurse her whenever there was a baby born or illness of any kind. My eldest sister had to stay at home whenever there was a new baby at the parsonage, and we took it in turns to take my mother's baby there for her to feed at the breast three or four times a day, for it generally happened that my mother had a baby dependent on her for the breast when our clergyman's wife had her babies. When my mother was away, my father gave out each morning before he went to his work the portion of food for each one of us for the day. We were all allowed a teaspoonful of sugar except 'baby Lizzie' – myself – who had a tea-spoonful and a half, much to my brother's disgust.

When I think of my poor overworked, tired mother I wonder that she lived as long as she did. She was kind-ness itself, the friend of everybody, and her own enemy, for her good nature was her downfall. She would get into debt to get nourishment for a sick neighbour or food for a family in distress. The worry of meeting all her liabilities and the continual grinding away at work for her own family and working outside her home, at last undermined her once splendid constitution. About the time I was nine years old, my mother used to be very poorly, and an old doctor advised her to take a little spirits. She was so often without money, and so often in want of a little drop of spirits, that I got into the habit of saving up all the pennies I earned running errands or minding babies, and when my mother had one of her poorly turns I would spend my money and fetch her the medicine I believed it to be. How little I knew what I was doing! My mother was everything to me; I always thought whatever she did or said was sure to be right, so naturally when she wanted drink and I had the means of getting it, the greatest pleasure in my life was to give her a pleasant surprise in the shape of a small quantity of gin. After several years of ill-health, she died. She was a good and kind mother, and as I think over what her life was, I feel she could not have done much better for her children than she did.

A short distance from my home a new neighbourhood had sprung up. People lived in six-roomed houses, and some kept little servants. Others who did not keep a girl in the house used to employ girls on Saturdays to clean their steps. A good many girls that I knew were what were called 'step girls' and earned what to me was a small fortune – about 9d. – on Saturdays cleaning people's steps. One Saturday I thought I would try my luck and see if I could earn some money, so off I went, unknown to anyone who would be likely to tell my mother. I had not been out long when it began to rain, spoiling all my chances of earning money. I knocked at several doors and asked if they would like the steps cleaned, but not one person would give me a job, so I had to give up in despair. One lady asked me if I was hungry; she said she was sorry she could not have her step cleaned, but if I waited she would give me something to eat. Presently she came to the door with a parcel and gave it to me, telling me not to waste any; what I could not eat I was to take home to my mother. I thanked her and ran off to a sheltered place to open the parcel, expecting to find something I could eat for I was very hungry. But I was doomed to disappointment, for the parcel contained some very dry pieces of bread and some crusts that looked as if they had been nibbled by mice, and a large piece of bacon rind. I could not eat any of it but had promised not to waste it so I gave the bacon rind to a hungry looking dog and carried the crusts to a man who kept a donkey. I had two things fixed in my mind. My mother was constantly telling us if we wanted to waste any of our food that 'wilful waste brings woeful want,' and my father repeatedly told his children never to promise unless they intended to keep their word.

Not very far from my home a very fine church was built, and attached to this church were a large number of Sisters of Mercy. Everyone was very concerned about this invasion of Sisters of Mercy in our neighbourhood and all kinds of rumours were afloat concerning them. Many uncharitable things and some good things were put down to their credit. As there was nowhere else but the streets for the children to play in, and children raced the streets long after it was dark, they got into all kinds of mischief, and all kinds of strange tales were told about the Sisters of Mercy, who had taken a large old-fashioned house in rather an out-of-the-way place. One of the good reports we had heard was that they had come to live among the people to be kind and good to them, so several girls about my own age made up their minds they would go one evening and ask for something to eat. I was one of the three who went to the door; I was then nine years old. A bigger girl than myself knocked at the door. When I saw the white-capped face through a grating in the door asking us what we wanted, I felt more like running away than asking for bread, but my companions did not seem inclined to run so I would not turn coward. The big girl asked for some food and the door opened. How frightened I felt! And how I wished I had never consented to take part in that bit of mischief! Two of us were asked to wait outside and the big girl was told to go inside. I don't know what we expected, but I don't think we ever hoped to see her again. We thought when that door closed she had gone from us for ever. We were wondering what we should have to tell her mother if we had to go home without her, when the door opened and she came out smiling with a packet of food in her hand. She said the Sisters had asked her a good many questions, and she had told them the truth about her family that was not generally known. They had spoken very kindly to her and had given us some cake to eat then, and would call to see her mother in the morning. What she had told the Sisters was that two of her sisters and her grandmother were very ill and that they were too poor to have a doctor. The family got their living by match-box-making, and when they had finished all the work they had in the house they would send for the parish doctor. The next morning two Sisters of Mercy came to visit the invalids. I don't think it ever was known how the Sisters knew there was illness in that house, but I remember my mother saying, 'Now they will be found out,' and found out the poor things were, for the Sisters went into the house and saw three persons, two children and an adult, all very ill with smallpox. No care was taken to prevent infection spreading. The match-boxes were being made in the same room as the people who had smallpox were lying in. The boxes were sent into thousands of homes, and who can say how many deaths were caused by poverty, for it was the want of money to buy food that caused these persons to keep on with their work while such an infectious complaint was in their home. The Sisters were more than kind to that family. With their help the invalids were properly looked after and work stopped till infection was over. I don't remember how long it was before they began to work at their trade again, but I do remember what a different feeling folks had towards the Sisters. The children, who had got some fantastic ideas regarding them, and who would run away when they saw them coming, would now wait for them to come along and would smile up into their faces in the expectation of getting a smile in return, and it was seldom they were disappointed. One day I went with a girl to take home some match-boxes. The match factory was at the back of a large old-fashioned mansion. At one time the neighbourhood was a very aristocratic part of the suburbs of London, but as the town grew the gentle-folk had gone farther out, so it came about that what was once a fine family mansion was now used for the family of the owner of the match factory, and what had been a coach-house and stables had been converted into a factory. The front of the house was beautifully kept. The windows always took my fancy because they looked clean and had nice curtains, the upper ones with brass bars on top of the short curtains, and the bottom ones with long lace ones. There was a large old-fashioned garden with bright flowers in the front of the house, with a large mulberry tree in the centre of a well-kept lawn, with seats under the lovely old tree. As we went past we saw three ladies sitting in the shade doing some kind of fancy work. We were rude enough to look through the fence to admire their pretty dresses, and were told to go about our business. What a contrast the back was to the front! It was a very hot day and the sun was shining just as much there as in the front, but there was no shelter from the sun's rays for the workers who had to stand there and wait their turn. There seemed to be a good many women and children waiting for some more work to be given out and their paltry earnings paid to them. Some were getting into trouble because they had only brought part of their work back. The girl I went with was one of the unfortunate ones. They all made reasonable excuses, but what was quite clear to my childish mind was that they all wanted the money for the work they had done to buy food for their dinners. Some had to plead very hard for their pay, and when it was given to them it was given with a rough word of warning that if the rest of their work was not done and brought in that night there would be no more work for them the next day, and that if they could not do the work there were plenty who could. While all this was going on in the yard I could see a servant who was very busy preparing dinner in the kitchen, and the delicious smell of roast meat came to the waiting workers. Several women passed remarks regarding the smell and wished they could be invited to dine off that joint. But that was too good for matchbox makers. Their diet consisted of fried fish and potatoes, or pease pudding and faggots, if they had earned enough to pay for such dinners; if not, bread and dripping with a glass of the cheapest beer. As I write this, I can see that house as I saw it on the day I am describing – the handsome old house with the garden with bright flowers and well-kept lawn and fine old mulberry tree on one side; on the other the hard-faced man giving out work and handing the small sums of money due to the sad-faced women and children, some of whom had scarcely any boots to their feet and very little clothing to cover them.

At the corner of the street was a baker who did a good business on Sundays. A good many people managed to get a piece of meat for the Sunday dinner. No one had a cooking stove so the meat and some potatoes and a pudding were all put into one dish and taken to the bakehouse to be baked. We used to arrive home from Church just as all the folk were fetching their dinners from the bakehouse. I have heard many complaints made about the baker robbing the poor people of some of their dinners; it was generally supposed that he took a little from each and in that way had a good dinner for himself. I remember one Christmas the mother of a poor family in the street did not take any dinner to the bakehouse, and it was found out afterwards that all they had for their Christmas dinner was a piece of bread and a pound of sprats. I could not get over the shock of anyone so near having such a miserable Christmas dinner and I worried my mother so much that at last I had to give up talking about it or get a thrashing. It is a good thing we are not permitted to look into the future, or I might have seen myself twenty years later without the means of getting even a pound of sprats for Christmas Day.

As time went on the close atmosphere told on my health and I was always ailing. At last the family doctor advised a change of air as the only chance of saving my life. My joy knew no bounds when I heard I was to go into the country. This was what I had longed for; I wanted to see the country I had heard so much about from my parents and had seen in pictures. I wanted to live in a country village, in a cottage with a thatched roof. I wanted to see cows in a real farmyard, not in a dirty place like the one at the back of our house. I wanted to play on clean ground, not on black ground such as our streets were made of. The longing for clean ground came to me through seeing my brother unpack his boots covered with yellow dust, and I remember as if it were only yesterday wondering whether all the roads were made up of dust like that on his boots, and the longing came over me to see those self-same roads. I would sit for hours by myself in my mother's bedroom making dolls' clothes out of a few pieces of material that a dressmaker gave me, but had no doll to put them on, till one day someone gave me a wooden Dutch doll. I did not care much for the doll, but I was able to fit on the clothes that I made, and I believe I began at that time to continue to make things out of odd pieces that no one else would have turned to account, a habit that has proved very useful to me all my life. While I sat and worked I would wonder how long it would be before I could go to the country, and often made my mother cross with my worrying to know. It seemed such a long while to wait. But before I could go and stay with my aunt, I had to be properly clothed, and clothes cost money, which was always scarce in my family. I can only remember a new pair of boots, a grey cape and a new frock made out of the lining of a dress that had been given to my mother by a former mistress she had lived with before marriage. At last the day came for me to go with my aunt. I had promised not to cry to come home when I got to my aunt's home. The idea of my crying to leave the country! Only let me get there, was my thought. Shall I ever forget the day when I left Bishopsgate Station, or the ride in the train?

The excitement of the whole time is quite fresh in my memory and the kiss from my mother, her anxious look at parting from me and her hope that the change would do as much for my health as the doctor anticipated, her instructions to my aunt regarding my health! At last we were off and I was on my way to the country that I had longed for! I had no idea how far we were going. I knew we were going to Cambridge and then, by a carrier's cart, to the village where my aunt lived. About half-way on the journey I was pushed under my aunt's crinoline and a man came to look at the tickets. I learnt years after that no ticket had been taken for me and that was why I had been hidden away, so I was a little stowaway, taken to the beautiful country by fraud. After we got to Cambridge after some little delay we started for the village and arrived there in the evening. The first thing that attracted my attention was the smoke curling up into the air out of the chimney of a cottage with a thatched roof, and the smell of burning wood was to me the most delightful scent that I had ever smelt. It had a real country smell, and even now, if I smell green wood burning, my mind carries me back to my first visit to the country. I have been to that village many times since and every time I get to that spot I almost unconsciously look for the blue smoke from the old chimney and quite expect to smell burning wood.

I spent five weeks in the country and lived out-of-doors most of the time. My uncle was farm bailiff and lived in a cottage on the estate, but it did not have a thatched roof, so I did not get all I wanted. I spent a great deal of time with my uncle. I went with him to fetch the cows in and stayed to see them milked. They were so tame that I often had a ride on their backs, and in time I could make them come to me in the field if I called them. I used to go in a cart with my uncle when he went to fetch food for the cows and waited while the men cut down the clover and other food, and came home perched on the top of the load. I was at first very frightened of the bees, but when I was told that if I was frightened of the bees I should have to go back to London I soon got over my fright or kept it to myself. In time I got used to the bees, and would wander around the hedges and would admire all the pretty wild flowers. There were some very fine trees just outside my aunt's window. The birds sang most delightfully in them, but the delight of my life was to watch the larks rise up out of a cornfield singing as if their throats would burst. The country was very flat but I remember what a lot of sky I could see and what delight-ful sunsets I could watch from the front of the house.

There were several children in the village I played with, and I had a chance of seeing inside several cottages with thatched roofs. I thought them very lovely then, but when I remember now some of the dilapidated dwellings called homes and think of all the inconvenience and lack of proper sanitation, I wonder that country folk are as healthy, mentally and morally, as they are. Two cottages that would make a lovely picture from the outside contained two rooms, one downstairs and one up. In one of these a man, his wife and four children lived. The room I used to go into to play with the little girl was small and dark; the window was very small; there was a door leading into the road and one to the back of the house and the staircase, all in the one room. I used to go as far as the school gate very often with some of my little playmates and wait for them when they came out of school. I wanted to go to school and asked my aunt to let me do so, but she said it was not worth while for a short time. I realised then I was only staying for a short time. Before then I never thought I was going back to dirty Bethnal Green, but now I knew my time in the country was coming to an end. The thought of leaving my aunt and uncle and all the animals, the clean yellow ground and the freedom made me very unhappy. I cried a good deal at first, but it was no good; a friend of my aunt's was coming for a few days and she was going to take me back to London and deliver me up to my mother. How I disliked that person! I put all the blame on her for me having to return to London. Why did she want a holiday? I did feel unreasonable about it, and even now when I hear the name of Griffith my mind goes back to the time when a Mary Griffith brought me back to London and the misery I felt when I saw the country receding and the town coming into sight.

2. Ten Years of Domestic Service.

When I was ten years old I began to earn my own living. I went to mind the baby of a person who kept a small general shop. My wages were 1/6 a week and my tea, and 2d. a week for myself. I got to work at eight in the morning and left at eight at night, with the exception of two nights a week when I left at seven o'clock to attend a night school, one of a number started by Lord Shaftesbury, called Ragged Schools. I was very happy in my place and was very fond of the baby, who grew so fond of me that by the time he was twelve months old he would cry after me when I went home to my dinner and when I went away to school before he was in bed. I felt very proud of my influence over my baby, and got into the habit of taking him home with me rather than let him cry. But I could not take him to school with me. As it was summer time and his mother could not keep him quiet, she offered me 3d. more a week to give up going to school and stay with the baby. This was a great trial to me. I did not like to feel the baby was crying and being neglected while I was at school. At the same time the teacher was so pleased with my progress and I was so anxious to learn, that I decided to stay at school. This upset my mistress and she made up her mind I should not go to that silly school. The conflict ended by my refusing to work for her, and so we parted. During the time I worked at that small shop I saw a great deal of the sad side of the lives of the people who lived in the neighbourhood. Men would often come in to buy their dinners – a pennyworth of bread and two ounces of German sausage, or twopennyworths of bread and cheese, and very often a pennyworth of bread with a hole made in it containing a halfpennyworth of treacle. Articles of clothing and household goods were brought and left, something like a pawnshop, only food was given instead of money in return for the goods, which would be redeemed when the poor things were able to pay the money. I had to make out small tickets for a good many of the things. I have seen a pair of children's boots left in pawn for a loaf of bread and a small quantity of butter. Babies' pinafores, frocks, saucepans, candlesticks and all kinds of articles have been brought to hold for food. The practice was illegal, so all articles had to be brought in when no one was about, and I was trained to help to smuggle things in. I was also allowed to serve small articles and was being carefully taught how to weigh bread. I was told when I put a piece of bread on the loaf as a makeweight I was to be sure to press it down, so that the scale went down. I was getting quite expert in the art of cheating in weight, and thought I was very clever, when one day my aunt who had come to see my mother saw me serving in the shop and watched to see how a young girl like me would manage to serve. She soon discovered that I had been taught to weigh bread to the disadvantage of the customer, and when I went home to dinner, she told me she had watched me through the shop window and had seen me cheat a poor woman. When she explained that perhaps I robbed a poor child of a slice of bread I felt so thoroughly ashamed of myself and so sorry that I had not thought of the wrong I was doing, that I was days getting over it. I was too young to tell my mistress about it, but I never gave short weight again.

When I was thirteen years old I went into service at Hampstead where I stayed twelve months. I had a very kind mistress and plenty of good food. I was fairly happy, but had to sleep in a basement kitchen which swarmed with black-beetles, and this made me very wretched at nights. I was only allowed out on Sundays to go to church. Sometimes I got a change by going on to the heath with the three children. The tie was almost too much for me at times, and on more than one occasion on a fine Sunday, instead of going to church, I went to see my married sister who lived about a mile away. This meant I had to run all the way there and back to enable me to stay for a very short time with my sister. It also meant that I should get into trouble if my mistress found out I had not been to church, so to save trouble I often had to tell a lie and say I had been, but there was always the risk of being asked what the text was.

During my time of service with that lady there was a confirmation at Christ Church, Hampstead. I was prepared for confirmation by the Rev. Bickersteth and confirmed by the Bishop of London. The confirmation classes were a real joy to me. Firstly, I got out to them, which was a change; secondly, the Rev. Bickersteth was exceedingly kind and, as far as I can remember, made no difference with his pupils; and thirdly, I was getting some instruction which I was always ready for. The whole business of confirmation had a very curious effect upon my mind. I found out that I was to take the full responsibility of the promises made in my name at my baptism. I looked up the baptismal service and found my godparents had promised three things in my name: first, that I should renounce the devil and all his works, etc.; second, that I should learn the Lord's Prayer, etc.; third, that I should be brought to the Bishop to be confirmed. I had no idea who my godparents were, so I asked my mother to tell me something about my baptism, for I was curious to know who had made such promises and had never in any way taken any interest in my spiritual welfare. I found that at the time of my baptism, my mother had been nursing the Vicar's wife, and during conversation had said she had four children who had not been christened. This neglect was pointed out as so serious that my mother made up her mind to get all four christened as soon as possible. So one day when the church was opened for service, my mother and her brood of four attended and we were all christened. My godmother I never knew, but my godfather I had reason to know was the caretaker at the schools I went to. He had offered to stand godfather for the lot, and this my mother accepted, as he was the only man available. The reason

I remember him is that he used to frighten the poor schoolchildren by swearing at them and throwing his broom, which on one occasion hit me and hurt me very much. At first, when I learnt what a responsibility I was to take at my confirmation, I felt I could not go through with it, and then I thought I had no longer any right to leave the responsibility with such a man as my god-father. So I was confirmed, but I never took the sacrament. My teacher or mistress could not persuade me, I felt I was not worthy. I have always refused to stand god-mother to any child; looking at the solemn promises made and the little chance of ever being able to carry them out has always made me feel shy of undertaking such a responsibility. And as a mother I would not ask anyone to make such promises for my child. It should be the responsibility of both parents.

At the age of fifteen I had my first experience of maternity nursing. I went to service at Kentish Town, where there were four children, and in a few months another baby was born. A few days after the birth of the child the mother died of puerperal fever. I shall never forget being called up into the bedroom to see my mistress just before she died, and I have often wondered why she died. She was quite a young woman and everything was clean, and there seemed no reason for her death. From that time till I left, two and a half years later, I had the principal care of the baby. I loved it as I love my life. I think it was at that time that I felt I should like to become a nurse. I knew nothing of the facts of life regarding childbirth, it all seemed so mysterious. I asked the woman who came to work questions concerning childbirth and her answers were so crude and very often disgusting. She seemed to look on the function of giving life as a joke. There was no one else I could speak to about the subject so I had to remain in ignorance, and I really cannot say how I did get my knowledge.

I had to work very hard, and very often was so tired with minding the children and doing housework that I have been found asleep on the stairs on my way to bed. My wages were very small, 3/- a week, and I often bought myself some food as I always felt I could eat more than was given to me. I tried to dress nicely, and to save expense managed to make my cotton dresses. This meant getting up early in the morning or sitting up late at night. My sister who worked at a factory always seemed to be better dressed than I was, and I suppose I envied her a little. One day I was tempted to do wrong. A gentleman who had seen me about with the children met me out alone one evening and offered me 10/- to go with him into a house for a short time. I thought of what 10/- would buy and how long I had to work for 10/-. And then I thought of my dear mother. Her poor tired face came into my mind and I felt that if I had been tempted to do wrong with the promise of £10,000, I would not for my mother's sake. I have had many temptations during my life, but my mother's face always seemed to stand between me and temptation.

After the death of my mistress her mother and sister came to take charge of the home and children. This made a great difference to me. My mistress used to teach her children instead of sending them to school. I had often to mind the youngest child while the mother in the same room taught the two elder children to read. In this way I learnt how to spell and pronounce a good many words. After the baby came, the children went to school, and as I had the principal care of the child, I had very little time to myself. If by chance I was seen reading, I was told that I ought to be able to find something better to do, and generally speaking a job was found for me. The result of this treatment caused me to read when I ought to have been doing my work. I managed to do so when I went upstairs to make the beds, etc. The servant next door lent me some trashy books that came out weekly. These books had tales that were continued week by week, and the tales were so arranged that they left off 'to be continued in our next' at a very exciting part of the story. This gave a young, impressionable girl a keen desire for the next chapter. After a while I became so fascinated with the tales that when the day came for the book to come out I had no peace of mind until I had been to the shop to get it and had found some means to read it. I don't quite know what made me give up reading the trashy things, I think it must have been thinking of my mother. I had heard my brother had been discharged from his employ-ment for reading whilst he should have been at work, and that my mother was upset about it. I was always anxious not to give mother any worry, so I think my brother's dis-charge helped me to break the bond that was holding me regarding reading, and I gave it up. It required a good effort, but I managed by not beginning a fresh tale. I have often thought how different my life at that time might have been if I had had a good book lent me to read and that I could have read it openly.

I left just before I was seventeen because of an injus-tice. I was allowed out from 3 to 5 o'clock one Sunday and from 6.30 to 9 the next, no time during the week.

One day the grandmother asked me what I did on Sunday afternoon. I told her I went for a walk. Then she said, if that was so I might as well take the children with me. This I considered unfair as I had to take them out all the week, and then was expected to take them out with me on my free day. She thought I was unobliging and I thought she was unjust, so we parted. I felt very bad at leaving the little child that I loved so much, but I could not stand injustice.

My next place was quite an improvement on all my previous ones and my life changed altogether. I went to live with a lady and her daughter. She had imposed three conditions on me if I entered her service. First, I was to take the pads out of my hair (large chignons being then the fashion); second, I was to cut the tail off my dress (long dresses were then worn); third, I was to wear aprons with bibs to them (which were never worn in those days). All three I objected to, but I finally agreed to cut off the tail of my dress and to put bibs to my aprons, but I would not take my hair down. I went in one night, feeling sure I should run away next morning. I was very miserable all day, everything was so different to what I had been used to. I missed the children I had to mind in my last place, and wondered how I could exist in such a quiet place with no one to speak to except when my mistress gave an order. I felt like a prisoner. Evening dinner was at six o'clock, after which I had nothing to do. I began to feel I must run out of the place and I really believe I should have done so, but just when I felt I could stand the loneliness no longer, my mistress came and asked me if I would like a run out for half an hour as she thought I must feel dull with no one to speak to. I very gladly accepted. It was then 7.30 and I was to be sure to be in by 9 o'clock. I had never had such consideration shown me before. All the time I was in that place I was always in to time; in fact it became a recognised thing for me to be in the road when the church clock struck nine.

In this household, reading was not considered a waste of time, and books were supplied to me to read which were suitable to a young impressionable girl, far different to the trash I had read in secret before. Then too, I was encouraged to improve my education. I used to write and my mistress would correct the mistakes in spelling and grammar. I also used to write to my brother who was a schoolmaster, and he would answer and return my letter corrected.

My love for the country was just as strong as ever it was, and as I had more time to myself now than I had ever had before I read books with descriptions of travels. A railway time-table with a map in it was quite an education to me. I used to trace the distance of different towns through which trains would have to go, and I learnt the names of all the most important villages and the counties they were in. In fact, I became quite a traveller in my mind. The people I lived with came from Manchester, and when I was quite a child, my father once went there and brought home pictures of Manchester Law Courts with him. I think this first started me wishing to go to Manchester, and if tracing the distance on the map and the knowledge of all the places I should have to pass through would have landed me there, I should have got there many years before I did, which was in July 1892, when the Women's Co-operative Guild celebrated the opening of its hundredth branch.

My father and I were great friends. We were the only ones in the family who were very fond of walking and whenever a chance came along, we set out for a good walk in the country. My father made notes of all the places we passed through, any particular spot that attracted our attention, the length of time we had walked, etc. In the winter when I went to see my parents, a map was brought out and my father and I traced our various journeys, and we talked over them, which gave us real pleasure. It was almost as good as going over the road again. Sometimes we walked twenty or more miles in a day.

I spent one of my holidays at home with my sister who was expecting her fifth child. I arranged to have my time off at the time of her confinement to look after her and the other children. I came in close touch with childbirth this time, as the doctor, who thought me much older than I was, asked for my help. I was terribly frightened, but I have never been a coward and did not intend to be one then, so I consented to help him if I was wanted. Fortunately I did not have much to do as the baby arrived without any trouble. I did all that I could for my sister and family with the help of an old woman who called herself a midwife. When I remember the methods adopted to carry out childbirth and the puerperal period in those days, it seems wonderful to me that so many mothers lived to bring a large family into the world. In some instances the poor unfortunate patient was not allowed to have her face and hands washed for days. I remember hoping I should never have a baby if I could not be washed. Then, after the trying ordeal they had gone through, they were not allowed to go to sleep for some hours. Their food consisted of water gruel and toast; milk was an unheard of thing.

At the age of eighteen, I was considered a fine strapping young woman. I had been in my place for a year and had been given a substantial rise in wages which enabled me to dress better and to save a little. I had quite changed my ideas of dress. At sixteen I had liked finery; at eighteen I had begun to like good material rather than shoddy finery. The dress I wore usually suited me, and I began to attract the young men. My sister got very annoyed with me for encouraging them and said I ought to be ashamed of myself. Then she got alarmed for fear something should happen to me and told my father of what she considered my folly. I did not try to prevent any of my male friends from taking me for a walk. I could not see any reason against it. No thought of evil came into my mind, but when each of my male friends wanted to monopolise all my time, then I realised that some of them were hoping for more than friendship. I had a direct offer of marriage from a widower who kept a public-house. He was very anxious to take me for his second wife. The lovely dresses and fine times I was to get if I would only consent to be wife No. 2! He was a friend of my sister's husband. Neither my sister nor her husband persuaded me either way. All the inducements held out failed to tempt me. I had once by accident gone into a church when a very grand wedding was going on, and I heard the promises made by the contracting parties. I came away with the idea that the woman had given up all her freedom, and that it required a great deal of love to induce a thoughtful woman to give up so much. The thought of what I should have to give up, and the want of any love for the man, made me refuse.

Later on, I became engaged to be married to one of my many admirers. I was engaged for about two years. In the meantime my mistress had sold her house and was going to live at Hastings. All through the winter I had to think about getting another place or getting married, but I was to go to Hastings first for a good holiday, as I was tired out with work. The idea of a month at the sea was delightful. I had never seen the sea. We went to Hastings in November and my stay lasted till April. I remember it was election day in Hastings. I knew nothing about politics; I did not even know what Liberal and Conservative meant. It puzzled me like nearly all things that I did not understand. I soon found out, and from that time till I got to understand the Labour Movement I was on the side of the Liberals.

As I was kept so long away from my future husband, my mistress invited him down for the day to see me, and paid all expenses. It was a beautiful day and we went for a long walk into the country. Here my engagement came to an abrupt end. The man that I had promised to entrust my future life to made improper suggestions to me, and when I refused tried to overcome me by force. I am thankful I succeeded in defeating him. From that moment I lost all respect for him and, in spite of all his protestations of regret and promises that it should not occur again, I told him I would never forgive him, and broke off the engagement there and then. I never told my mistress what had taken place, I think I was too ashamed. When we went back to Hampstead, I used to go out as usual, and every time I met him he pleaded for forgiveness. At last I could bear it no longer, and asked my mistress to let me leave. She knew I was in trouble with my love affairs, but never tried to force my confidence. So with regret she let me try to find another place. I went to live at Balham, hoping I should be far enough away, but he found me out, and after six months coming to see me every time I went out he got tired and gave up his hopeless task of winning me back.

3. Married Life, Midwifery, Co-operation.

It was at a mission hall, where I went when I found the church too stiff and conservative, that I met my husband. We were both keenly interested in social problems. It was he who interested me in free education. Many of the elder married people were much concerned because they had had to pay school fees for their own children, and now they said they had got to pay a rate to educate other people's. My own father said so. I was engaged for three years before we were in a position to settle down, and then when everything was fixed up, rooms taken, furniture bought, arrangements made for the wedding to take place, the piano-making firm my husband worked for went bankrupt and he was thrown out of work. We decided not to put off the wedding, hoping he would soon find other work, and we were married on December 2nd, 1882, he being twenty-seven and I twenty-six years of age.

For eight months my husband tramped from early morn till late at night looking for work, and during all that time he did small jobs which brought in £3 in all. The little money I had saved had dwindled down to a few pounds. I had tried to help the situation by first going out to work and then by doing washing at home. I turned my hand to anything that would honestly bring in money. My health was becoming impaired with work and worry and I was expecting a baby which made it very hard for me. But I made the best of what every one of my friends called a bad job, and like Mr Micawber was always hoping for something to turn up. It did at last, just a month before my baby was born. My husband got a job on the Midland Railway as carriage cleaner at St. Pancras. He worked on nights, twelve hours a night, six nights a week, at the large wage of 19/- a week. It was very dirty work, but we were thankful for that amount of money, for I was beginning to wonder how my confinement was to be paid for when I had to give up work. I was also very anxious about the health of the coming baby. I knew enough about maternity to know I had not had sufficient food to nourish myself and child, and then I felt the great responsibility of bringing a new life into the world, I used to worry myself a good deal and wonder whether I should make a good mother. But I prayed that I might make a worthy mother and that the child might be strong and healthy, and that I should be able to bring it up well.

My baby, a boy, was born on September 3rd, 1883. I

had rather a bad time as I had to be delivered with forceps and had nothing to lull the pain, so had to feel all that was going on. The baby was small and puny and very cross. I had no one with me after the morning and had to depend on the neighbours. My husband did what he could, but he had to sleep in the daytime and I was always all alone at night. I was up at the seventh day, but I took care to do no more than I could help. When my baby was three months old my husband lost his job, and was out of work again. When he came home and told me I did not know what to do. I was weak and my baby was cross and poorly. I had never given in with all the previous troubles but now I could not help giving way. I had never parted with any of my clothes or furniture by pawning, as I had been advised to many times by kindly folk who thought they were suggesting a good thing for hard times. I had always managed without, but now I could see my things going, for I could not work with a young baby even as I had done before he was born. However, it was not so bad as I had anticipated, for a man who lived in the same house told my husband to go after a job at St. Pancras Station. He said it would be less money but it was better than nothing. He got the job as porter on the bank, which meant loading and unloading trucks, all night work at 17/- a week. My rent was 7/- a week, club 8d. a week, and I was obliged to pay 1/3 a week for fares for my husband to ride one way to his work. We lived six miles from St. Pancras and it was impossible for him to walk both ways and work the long hours which constituted a night's work. The long hours and heavy work told on him, and when winter set in he was taken ill and was ill for a long time. Then I had only 12/- a week club money. From that time till he died, I am sure he had on an average six months' illness every year. I was very poor but no one outside my door ever knew how often I was hungry or how I had to scheme to get my husband nourishment.

My baby grew into a strong, sturdy little fellow, full of mischief. It was a great treat to look after him and help to earn the living. At the same time it meant taking him out in the daytime and working after my husband had gone to work at night. Many times till 4 o'clock in the morning in bitter cold weather I have been washing, and have just been able to get two hours' sleep before the child woke up, which he did about 6 o'clock. My second child, a boy, was born three years later. By that time my husband's wages had risen to £1 1s. a week, and he worked nearer home which was a little better for me. My baby was delicate from birth and was ill for some months before he died. I was insufficiently nourished during pregnancy and nearly lost my life through want of nourishment and attention at my confinement and lying-in period. I think if it had not been for a good neighbour I should have gone under.

When my husband's wages reached the magnificent sum of £1 1s. a week, he joined the Railwaymen's Trade Union. At first I thought 5d. a week a lot of money for what I considered very little benefit. I did not understand the principle of the Trade Union Movement, but I have since had cause to be thankful that my husband joined a Trade Union. For twenty-six years I paid all subscriptions, and willingly paid a levy of 1/- a year for political purposes, believing it to be one of the ways the workers could emancipate themselves, and I have done my best to get members into Parliament, not by speaking in public but by working in any way I could.

Soon after my husband joined his Trade Union, a Co-operative Store was formed at Child's Hill. I gave my husband the necessary 1/6 to join. There, I thought, was a chance of getting something back. I had been told about the wonderful dividend and the interest on share capital, but nothing about the principles that should govern the Co-operative Movement. In fact, I thought the Child's

Hill Society stood alone. I was so interested in getting the 'divi.' that I walked two miles to the Store every time I wanted a few things. My shilling soon grew into a pound and I began to think I was eating myself into a banking account. I put a few shillings on to my share capital and I felt that I should have a few pounds in time for a rainy day. Alas! my hopes were all blighted. By the time I had managed to save £12 the Society failed, and I lost every penny with the exception of 1/8 which was my share of what was left. It was a great blow to me at the time, but, remembering the old saying, 'what can't be cured must be endured,' I set to work to endure the loss as cheerfully as I could. During the time the Society was in existence, an Education Committee was formed and through them a Branch of the Women's Co-operative Guild. Now, in looking back, I can truthfully say that, although I lost £12 in money through the break-up of the Society, I gained far more than £12 worth of knowledge, and my life was brightened to such an extent that everything seemed changed. The Education Committee arranged lectures on all kinds of subjects which I used to attend, and the lectures gave me the knowledge I so badly needed. Then one day my husband brought me two tickets for a tea and social which he asked me to use. I could not very well spare the time, but I did not like to waste the tickets for I knew it was a big sacrifice out of my husband's little bit of pocket money. So I managed to go and take a friend with me. We had a nice tea, some songs and speeches, and then, after a speech by Miss Llewelyn Davies, names were taken to form a branch of the Women's Co-operative Guild. I was asked to join but told them I could not as I was far too busy. I thought a meeting in the middle of the week was quite impossible. I still had to wash and iron for my living. However, the old lady who had been so kind to me at my confinement gave my name in, and explained to me afterwards that she thought it would do me good to go to a meeting once a week and leave my worries behind me for a few hours. She also told me she thought I might be useful in a meeting of this kind. I joined the Guild and found the benefit my neighbour had predicted. It meant a long walk to the meeting and back, something fresh to listen to while there, and something to think about all the week. I was not used to working-women managing their meetings. I had attended Mother's Meetings, where ladies came and lectured on the domestic affairs in the workers' homes that it was impossible for them to understand. I have boiled over many times at some of the things I have been obliged to listen to, without the chance of asking a question. In the Guild we always had the chance of discussing a subject. The Guild was more to my mind than the Mothers' Meeting, so I gave up the Mothers' Meeting and attended the Guild.* I had only been a member ten months when I was elected President, and from that time till I came off the National Central Committee in 1922, I was in office of some kind.

When I had been a Guild member about a year, I took up a share in my own name. I had learnt in that time that women should take an active part in the Co-operative Movement and that they should attend quarterly meetings of their Societies. That was the reason I took up a share. I was nominated for a seat on the Management Committee by a very progressive man who thought me a

---

*Another Guildswoman wrote: 'I used for a short time to attend a Mothers' Meeting, and did so more from a point of duty than anything, but after joining the Guild I did not feel to have patience to listen to the simple childish tales that were read at the former, and did not like to feel we had no voice in its control. There is such a different feeling in speaking of trials and troubles to Guilders (where they are real) than to speak to the ladies of the Mothers' Meeting. You know that they have a fellow-feeling being all on an equality, but there is the feeling in speaking to the ladies that after consulting this one, that one and somebody else, a little charity might be given – the tradesman perhaps who has always had your custom in better circumstances, he knows all about your business when you present your charity ticket. This sort of thing to honest working people hurts their feelings of independence, but when co-operators help them it is done in a different way.'

woman with some common sense, but there was such a storm at the idea of a woman on a Management Committee that I did not seek election, and the members put my husband on instead.

I shall never forget the first time that I had to go from the Guild to the Management Committee to ask for some money to help on the Guild work. No one would go with me, they were all too nervous. I was nervous too, but I did not let anyone know it till I got into the Committee room and stood behind my husband's chair. Then he knew it, for I nearly shook him off his chair. I attended nearly all the Guild Conferences, which were often held on a Thursday, the end of my financial week. I have walked six miles to a Conference and back because I had no money to pay fares. I was at the first Conference Miss Spooner ever came to, held over a Store in City Road. We were trying to arrange a Guild programme that would suit our Guild members. Domestic economy and cookery were suggested, and as a result of that meeting I was asked to seven different Guilds and gave what they chose to call a 'lecture' on Economical Cookery!

Then I went to a conference at Leman Street when Miss Holyoake (now Mrs Holyoake Marsh) gave an address on Trade Unions for Laundry Workers. I expressed some of my objections to some of her remarks to a fellow delegate. The speaker said that anyone could set up a laundry with a few clothes-pegs, a line and a pail. Of course I objected to that, and said that proper appliances were needed – washtubs, copper, irons, soda, a proper place, etc. My fellow delegate almost pushed me up on to my feet to make me say out what I had said to her, which I did, and all the delegates agreed with me. I have since reminded Mrs Holyoake Marsh of the incident, it being my first speech in public. She remarked that if she did no other good that afternoon, she made me speak!

When my husband was promoted to the position of under-guard, we had to leave Brondesbury and come to Cricklewood to live. Then it was I gave up washing and took up nursing. My husband's wages had now risen to £1 3s. a week, and he had an allotment. I got a nice little flat for 7/- a week, so that I did not live a life of drudgery, but had to do something to help. The chance of nursing came to me through one of the members of our Management Committee, who advised his master to come for me when his wife was ill, saying, 'She is not a nurse but I am sure she will do, and be kind to your wife.' I did what I could and satisfied both patient and doctor, who recommended me to others of his patients. My first maternity case came to me in an unexpected manner. One of our Guild members was expecting her confinement and could not find a nurse. So at last I got a crippled girl I knew to stay in my house while I went into the Guild member's house, and acted as maternity nurse for a fortnight. I did not intend to take up maternity nursing, but after I had started, other Guild members came to me to attend them. I began to like the work, and the doctors were so satisfied with me that I determined to keep on. Then several doctors advised me to go in for midwifery, but I could not go into hospital for training. The fees were a bar to me. I found that the cheapest training I could get would cost anything from £30 to £50, and then I should have to be away from home for three months. This was quite impossible for my husband's health needed all the care I could bestow on it to keep him anything like fit for work part of his time. I had no money, only as I earned it week by week, and it was impossible to save. So I had to content myself with being a maternity nurse, but I always hoped I should ultimately become a midwife. I read and asked questions of the doctors and in this way knew a great deal about the theory of midwifery, and I was gaining experience in the practical part. There were three doctors who were very good to me and were willing to lend me books or to teach me anything. I was taught to deliver with forceps, which midwives are not taught in hospitals. I went to several post-mortems with a doctor. One was the case of a young girl who was pregnant and had poisoned herself. The doctor opened the womb and let me see the dear little baby lying so snugly in its mother, and gave me a lot of information that was real knowledge to me, showing me things in the human body which were both interesting and instructive.

Quite a large number of young married people came to live in Cricklewood, and I had sometimes as many as a hundred cases in a year. The doctors left so much to me and did so little for their fees, that people asked me to take their cases without a doctor. I did not care to do so at first, so I asked a doctor (who, when he thought my husband had not many days to live, had promised him to help me) if he thought I should be right to take cases without a doctor. He told me I was quite all right, and that if at any time I came across a case that I was not sure was quite straightforward, he would come to my assistance. I was very pleased with his offer and did many cases on my own responsibility, and both patients and doctors were satisfied, but I was not. I was called a midwife, but I felt I should have liked a hospital training, and

as I earned more money I began to save to get the training I longed for. I scraped and saved, twisted and turned
clothes about, even went as far as to turn an overcoat for
my husband. I managed to save £30, and got the necessary papers which had to be signed by a doctor. When I
went to him, he positively refused to sign it. He said it
would be a wicked waste of money, that I knew more
than the hospital would teach me, that I could not be
spared from the neighbourhood for three months, and
advised me to give up the idea. I gave up the idea. I had
gone without the necessaries of life to save the £30, and
I felt that if I was to get no benefit from the expenditure
on training I might keep and use it for something else. I
don't think I should have taken his advice if I had known
that the Midwives' Act was coming along. The doctors
trained me and sent me up for examination in midwifery.
But alas! I failed, as about 130 did at the same examination. The written examination took place at 9 p.m., in
a closely packed room. We had two hours to answer the
questions, and a fortnight later an oral examination. It
was just five minutes past 10 p.m. when I went into the
examiners' room; at ten minutes past I came out with a
slip of paper to give the Secretary with the word 'failed'
written on it. I was told I could pay another fee and go

through another exam, but I refused to do so. I was always a little nervous when writing or answering questions, and when I had to do both in a room full of doctors, I felt I should not make a better job of another exam. When the Midwives' Act became law, I was recommended for a certificate as a *bona fide* midwife. I have never let anyone see my certificate.

From the beginning of my Guild career I worked heart and soul in its cause. It meant hours and hours of careful study to get true facts to speak on. I was so afraid of being tripped up, I think I have written miles of paper in my time, working up a subject. At one time I won the prize given by the Co-operative Union for an essay on 'The Child and the State,' which enabled me to go to the Union's Summer School at Folkestone.

I had got so used to the Co-operative method of trading that when my Society failed I felt like a fish out of water. When another Society was started in Willesden, I joined it at once, and a Woman's Co-operative Guild Branch was soon opened also, and I was elected President. Later I was elected on to the Management Committee of the Society, and I am proud of the fact that I was the first woman my Society had ever sent to represent them at a Co-operative Union Congress. I don't think anyone at that Congress felt their responsibilities more than I did. There were several things that had to be voted on that had to be left to the judgment of the delegates and which called for a lot of careful consideration on my part, I was so anxious to do right. I was pleased when I gave my report that my Committee were satisfied. I was sent again as a delegate to Congress to Swansea, and gave my vote in favour of Co-operative politics.

One of the Co-operative lectures I heard was on the Co-operative Building Society and how Co-operators could buy their own houses. I was very interested in the scheme and always hoped I should be able to buy a house of my own, but how I should ever get the capital necessary to enable me to borrow money for the purchase of a house I did not know. When the doctor told me it was unwise to spend £30 on training, I took up five £10 shares in the Co-operative Building Society. It took me another ten years to save enough to borrow the money to purchase a house. At that time I attended a course of L.C.C. lectures on Health and Sanitation and so got to know about drainage, damp courses, ventilation, etc. So I decided to have a house built with all the latest drainage, etc., and I surprised the builder very much with my suggestions. I got a good house, or rather two self-contained flats. When the war was in progress and rents and rates and taxes went up, I did not put up my rents. I had good tenants, and I felt they had helped to buy the house for me and were entitled to a little consideration.

The education I got in the Guildroom made me understand more about the laws of the country. So when I was ready to buy my house I had put the mortgage in my name. This caused a little friction between my husband and myself. He thought that although I had earned and saved the money, the house should certainly be bought in his name. He said it did not look respectful for a woman's name to be put on the deeds when she had a husband alive. I thought different, and so the house is mine.

Sometimes my husband rather resented the teachings of the Guild. The fact that I was determined to assert my right to have the house in my name was a charge against the Guild. The Guild, he said, was making women think too much of themselves. I did not quite agree with him there, though I did and still do think the Guild has been the means of making its members think more of themselves than ever they did before. The Guild's training altered the whole course of my life. When I look back and think what my life might have been without its training and influence, I shudder. I was living in a house with two other families whose only ideas in life were work and sleep, and, for recreation, a visit each evening to the public-house or a cheap music hall. They tried very hard to induce me to go with them, and possibly, if I had not been connected with the Guild, when my baby died I might have fallen a victim to the drink habit. It is impossible to say how much I owe to the Guild. It gave me education and recreation. The lectures I heard gave me so much food for thought that I seldom felt dull, and I always had something to talk to my husband about other than the little occurrences of daily life. Then I learnt in the Guild that education was to be the workers' best weapon, and I determined if it were to be at all possible that my son should have as good an education as I could give him. From a shy, nervous woman, the Guild made me a fighter. I was always willing to go on a Deputation if there was a wrong to be righted, or for any good cause, local or national.

My experience as a midwife was very useful when the Guild had the campaign for the National Care of Maternity. I am always proud of the fact that I was invited to speak on the first deputation connected with it. This was to get Maternity Benefit included in the Insurance Act. We were received by Sir Rufus Isaacs, in the place of Lloyd George. I explained the way in which women paid for their confinements. If a woman had a good husband, he gave her all he could from his wages, and the woman had to do the rest, going short herself, as the man had to be kept going for the work's sake, and it would break her heart to starve her children. Sir Rufus Isaacs asked me how much I thought a fair sum would be on which the woman could get through her confinement. I told him that nothing less than £5 would see her through comfortably. He said such an amount was impossible, and suggested the 30/- which was what the Hearts of Oak gave.

Later on, the L.G.B. offices were crowded one day by mothers with their babies, an unusual sight for Whitehall! They came to ask Mr Herbert Samuel to recognise that, during the war, the care of maternity was more important than ever. I specially pressed for Home Helps, and I told of how one of my patients was left alone in the house for two days at her confinement, with a little child of three in her bedroom. The child ran downstairs and poured paraffin on the fire and screamed with fright at the result. The mother ran down the landing in nightdress and no shoes. No mother should be left alone at such times. We were photographed afterwards on the steps of the L.G.B.

In 1917 I spoke on a deputation to Lord Rhondda at the Local Government Board, when every section of the Guild was represented. The deputation put before him a large scheme for the National Care of Maternity, and each Guildswoman had her special point, one Welsh-woman telling Lord Rhondda of what went on in his coalfields, and no one overlapped. He said he could only give us half an hour, but he listened very patiently for an hour and a half. At the end he said he would put the points before the Cabinet, and said he had no idea there was such a well-organized body of working-women as the Women's Co-operative Guild.

Another important deputation I went on during the war, and when, owing to weather conditions, I was the only one to attend with Miss Bondfield and had to do all the talking for the Guild, was to the Executive of the Prince of Wales' Fund, which had decided not to give relief to unmarried mothers. The Guild thought this was a very wrong policy, and asked the Executive to receive a deputation from the Guild to explain the reasons why they asked for that restriction to be removed. Miss Bondfield explained to me that the reason why the Committee had refused help to the unmarried mother was because some of the clerics of the Committee were of opinion that, if the unmarried mother was assisted from the fund, the feelings of all the respectable married women would be outraged. I told the Minister that, as a midwife, I had only the day before attended a respectable married woman and, knowing I had to go next day to plead the cause of unmarried mothers, my patient, so that I should not be late, had sat up in bed to wash herself, and was quite willing to let me leave her child unwashed until I could return. I explained that I represented the Women's Co-operative Guild, an organization 30,000 strong, chiefly composed of respectable married women, and that the Guild entirely repudiated the statement that married women would be resentful. I was asked a whole lot of questions, and, in asking them to reconsider their decision and give help to unmarried mothers, asked them not to forget that every time a woman fell, a man fell also. I said that when a recruiting sergeant asked young men to join up, he did not ask if they were married or unmarried, but only if strong and healthy and fit to go, and I also put in from the hygienic point of view that children of unmarried mothers were stronger and healthier. Mr Walter Long nudged Mary Macarthur and said, 'She's rubbing it in to us.' It was decided before we left the room to treat the unmarried mother with the same consideration as the married mother.

Three years after the war, when I was Vice-President of the Guild, the General and Assistant Secretaries retired, and I had the honour and pleasure of presenting them with the Freedom of the Guild, and of pinning a medallion on the breast of the General Secretary, Miss Llewelyn Davies. The presentation made me feel quite ill. I felt I was performing my last service to the Guild I had worked for and loved so well, and when I found myself out of office I felt lost. However, I soon found something to do. My Society was in very low water. The Share Capital had been tied up and written down 3/4 in the pound. This had a very bad effect on trade, and the Management Committee wrote to the Guild Branches and asked them to start clothing clubs in their Guild rooms, which was done with good results. I felt it needed wider scope than the Guild rooms, so I started a clothing club on my own responsibility and was responsible for every pennyworth of goods the members had from the Society. I paid for every voucher before I gave it out, and I am glad to say that, during the three years I ran the club, the Society did well over £1,000 worth of trade through it for ready money, and I only lost £2 in debts. I received a small commission and, in canvassing the members, I was able to smooth a good many ruffled feelings. It gave me an opportunity of speaking of the principles of the Co-operative Movement. The first week I started my club I took £1; it gradually increased till up to the present time I have taken in fifty-seven weeks £670. I have got men in my club who have never saved a shilling in their lives before. They save up for a new suit of clothes, and when they get them they are more than pleased and recommend others and go on saving for other things. It was very hard work, and at times I got very discouraged and wondered if all the time and trouble was worth it. Then the late Mrs B. Jones' face would come into my mind, and I could almost hear her saying, 'Try to leave the world a little better than you found it.' I thought the one way I could do this would be through Co-operation, and I would go on again. A few years later, the Society was amalgamated with the London Co-operative Society, when the members' capital regained its full value of 20/- in the £.

During the last years, events of great interest to me were the international meetings of Cooperative Guildswomen which were now being held. I have been to three of these – at Basle, where I read a paper on the Guild, at Ghent and at Stockholm, and I have paid my own expenses. How I managed to get money together is by being very careful in small things. As an example, instead of buying a new coat and hat, I turned my old one and blacked my hat with ink, and have generally patched and darned and twisted my clothes about, so that I have spent very little on new clothes. Then during the war I learned to repair boots, and now I repair my own. Then I have an allotment and manage to grow vegetables for myself, and sometimes have some to sell for Guild or hospital funds. I have managed all the work on my ground for thirteen years, but have been obliged to get a man to do the digging for the last two years. I have a very nice little hut and can rest and read and do a bit of sewing between planting, hoeing, weeding, etc. I lined the hut with paper and put up pictures. I have a stove on which I can cook a dinner, and a paraffin stove for heating. Very often I spend long days on my allotment, and cook quite nice little dinners of, say, a breast of mutton and peas and fruit off the allotment for myself and a friend who has been ill for a long time, and who is now reaping the benefit of the quiet and fresh air. She is a Guild member so we have a great deal in common to talk about. Often, to bring her out, we plan a little speech or paper on, say, washing and wash-houses (washing day is an abomination in every house) to be spoken or read at our own branch meetings. The little hut, where we sit and talk outside on chairs, is quite a picture, covered all over with ivy. I love to watch the things grow. Just at the present time everything looks so fresh. The seeds I put in are just beginning to peep through. There is a railway bank at the end of the path covered with grass and beautiful dandelions. I can sit outside the little shed and see the church tower of old Hampstead Church and think of all the good work that has been done in the Guild Office. I go there all day on a Sunday, and am sure there is as much spiritual feeling going along a ditch as there is in hearing a sermon. It is a nice change from my one little room where I live by myself, and do all there is to do, washing included. I have now got my old age pension and have given up my work as a midwife. With my pension and a little money I have saved and with commission on the mutuality club, I live very comfortably, and thank God that I became a Guild member for more reasons than I can explain.

A Plate-Maker's Wife

By Mrs Wrigley

I go back to the age of six, when I remember well falling in the canal, and was nearly drowned had it not been for my Sunday-school teacher. Strange to say my father saved her from being drowned in the very same place when he was a young man.

I was born in Cefn Mawr (Wales), April 17th, 1858. My father was a shoemaker, and worked for his brother Jonathan Jones. He made the late Sir Watkin Williams Wynn's Wellington boots. It was all hard work in those days. My father's earnings was 12s. per week, and there was five children. My mother went out day sewing for 1s. a day, when she could have work. I being the older one had to look after the other children. When mother was at home I had to go out and gather coal and cinders to make a fire, and walk two miles to a pit bank to pick coals, and carry it in a basket on my head. I also had to go two miles to a farmhouse for buttermilk; we could have as much as we could carry for 2d., ten to twelve quarts it was mostly. Our food then was potatoes and bacon, red herrings and bread and milk. There was no such thing as tea for the children in those days. Clear water we had to carry on our heads from some spring well. I remember one time my mother had been out sewing all day from eight to eight, and I had gone to bed with the others, as my father said I could. But when mother came in there was no clean water for breakfast, so she made me get out of bed and go through a wood for some clean water. I am not saying what my other sister said, but she thought my mother very cruel. At that time I went out cleaning the floors and back-yards on a Saturday for a penny a time, and a piece of bread and butter. I also carried dinners and suppers to the iron forge for twopence a week.

Some of the happiest days of my childhood were when my mother packed us off with food for the day with other children, and to take the clothes to wash. Then, by the River Dee, we would take a bucket full of coal and get a few boulder stones and make a fire to boil the clothes in the bucket, and rinse them in the river, for there was plenty of water and we hadn't to carry it. Then, while the clothes was drying we had a good romp. We would take the babies with us as well, for there was plenty fields for them to pick the little daisies, and the older ones looked after the little ones. Some of our parents would come down to see if we was all right, and then we would fold the clothes and go home singing and rejoicing that we had had a good washing day and a good play.

All this was when I was about eight years old. When I was about nine, the Vicar of the Church asked if I would go to be with his children and take them out. There was another servant, but I did not stay long, for we were rationed with our food and everything was locked up. My mother was glad for me to go out for food alone.

I had been at home a few days when the doctor's wife came to our house and said a lady and gentleman wanted a little nurse for their child, to go back with them to Hazel Grove, near Stockport. My little bundle of clothes was packed up and I went in full glee with them. Instead of being a nurse I had to be a servant-of-all-work, having to get up at six in the morning, turn a room out and get it ready for breakfast. My biggest trouble was I could not light the fire, and my master was very cross and would tell me to stand away, and give me a good box on my ears. That was my first experience of service life. I fretted very much for my home. Humble as it was, it was home. Not able to read or write, I could not let my parents know, until a kind old lady in the village wrote to my parents to fetch me home from the hardships I endured. I had no wages at this place, only a few clothes.

My next situation was on a farm where they kept 150 milking cows, near to Oswestry. It was there where I learnt to milk and make cheese and butter. I was very happy there looking after the calves, ducks, hens and chickens, and gathering the eggs. My wage was 2/6 per month. I stayed there until I was twelve years old. Then I went to another farm in Marple, where I was very comfortable and happy. My wages there was 3/- per month. I had five cows to milk morning and night, clean the shippens out, take the cows to the field and churn the butter in the afternoon, and four little children to look after while my mistress was busy in the shop. It was in the time of the great flood at Marple in 1871.

My third situation was in Oldham in 1872, at a Temperance Hotel. I was then fourteen years old. Seeing as I could not read or write, my master and mistress took an interest in me and paid for my education at the night school for two years. He also helped me at night with my lessons. They proved a father and mother to me. I was with them until I was nineteen years old, and I have a great deal to be thankful for in their kindness. They have passed away now, but I see their sons very often. My wage was 16/- per month, and was raised to 20/- per month before I left.

I had a little holiday at home, and got another place at Dobcross, Saddleworth, for a little more money. It was a big house and I worked very hard from morning till night. There was a big family and I did all the washing. I was not allowed out only on Sunday afternoon and one Sunday night a month. When a girl can go out and have a little freedom her work does not feel half the trouble to her. It was one Sunday afternoon at school I first saw my husband, and when my mistress got to know, she stopped me going out altogether. I wonder if the girls of to-day would stand that! I stayed with them two years until I was twenty-one, when I left for a better place.

Here there was four servants, and I was engaged for the cook. It was a real gentleman's house. They kept coachman, farmer and gardener, the very best place I had in all my life. We had plenty of freedom, going out in our turn. We were not treated as servants but as all one family, and the children was taught to treat us kindly and with respect. The servants was thought so much of, and when we had a ball the kitchen staff was allowed to have one dance with the guests. My master and mistress was real Christian and she was the kindest lady in the village. Everybody was alike to her, but she had her house rule kept in order. Not one of us was allowed out one minute after nine o'clock. The bell rang out 'all in,' but the girls loved her too much to disobey her. I was there five years, and married from there. I was sorry to give up such a good home, and they was sorry for me to leave, but my young man wanted to get married for he had no mother. I had a good send-off with many presents.

My husband was only a platelayer on the line and his wages was 18/- per week. Out of that he had 1/- for his pocket, and 1/- for tobacco, and 7d. for his Provident Club and pension, leaving me with 15/5 to carry on. Out of that I paid 2/8 rent, 1/4 for coal and lamp-oil, which cost 6d. then for three quarts, leaving me with 10/11 to live on for the week. I could not go out working, for I had never been in a mill. I did a little plain sewing to help us during the week to keep out of debt. We struggled along to get a nice home together, with my little sewing money. My first thing to do was to join the Co-operative Stores in one of the Oldham branches, and I am glad to say I have been a member for forty-six years. I cannot say how it has helped with my little children.

I had been married five months, when I found out my condition, and to prepare for that time, I took more sewing in, and worked night and day to save a little, working the machine and washing, anything to save a shilling or two. Just a week before my baby came, I made eight print tight-fitting jackets for 1/4 each, to get a little more to what I had saved. I had to suffer for it after. I went about with a little pillow under each arm for three months with gathered breasts. I had a very good neighbour, she helped me all she could, but mother had to come to take me home to get better. While I was away, my husband was taken ill, and I nearly lost him. I am glad to think women are better looked after in these days.

I remember one of my old neighbours. She was in a very poor way, hadn't much to live on, her husband being a gasser in a mill, and had 18/- per week. There was five children to keep and her rent 4/- per week. Day after day she went out washing and cleaning and taking washing in. Sometimes she run into debt for groceries, and her husband got very cross with her. She told me herself that she had gone without many a meal for the children and her husband, still he worried her for going into debt. She could not pledge, for there was nothing to pledge; it was a poor home. Her husband was a steady man, but the same as other men – went out and left her to it to do as she liked. She could not sew or mend for the children as she would like, and they had to go with very little on their backs. She went cleaning for two ladies that lived not far from here. These ladies went away for the summer months, and left her in charge of the house to put fires in. In a lumber-room there was a marble timepiece. She did not know what to do for the next meal. She took the timepiece and pledged it for a few shillings, with the intention to take it back before they came home. But the ladies returned sooner than was expected. They missed the timepiece and wanted to know where it had gone to. She told them all about it and how sorry she was to have to do such a thing. The ladies gave her so many hours to bring it. Her husband knew nothing about it, and at ten o'clock that night she was locked up all night and her five children in bed. Her husband could do nothing till next day. His master lent him money to pay the cost. The neighbours turned against her, and I felt so sorry for her I took them some food in as she was fretting very much. In a few days she sent for me and there was the baby born, and only a little boy in the house. I sent for the nurse, and I took some bed-clothes, made her bed, and looked after her until she was well, and washed her clothes. She has never forgotten what I did for her. The baby is a fine young man twenty-two years of age.

When we left Mossley to come to Stockport in 1894, I had three children. My husband was promoted, and his wages raised from £1 1s. to £1 2s. a week. At the time my fifth boy was born, he was having 26/6 to keep us all, and no children at work. I have seen the day when my white tablecloth and clean empty pots were waiting for father to bring his wages, before we could have something to eat, for I would not go to a little shop as I got better value for my money at the Co-operative Society, and there was something at the end of the quarter for clothes. I was feeling myself after my eldest boy began to work for 5/- per week. When the next came to work for another 5/-, and the next went out with newspapers, while the fourth boy, only young, delivered milk, I began to get on my feet, and with making all their clothes it was a great help. It was then I was determined to let them have music-lessons in their turn. I am glad to think now that we did our best for our children. I have gone without my dinner for their sakes, and just had a cup of tea and bread and butter.

Our ideas for our children was to give them the best education, a trade and music, that we could afford, so that they would grow up to be clean, honest, truthful, and to go straight in life and become good citizens. Each boy as he became fourteen years of age, was put to a trade of his own choosing. Their trades was as follows:

George, brick-archer (railway).
William, shoemaker (master).
Lewis, tin-plate worker.
Reggie, groceries, Co-operative (now Manager).
Osborne, locomotive fireman.

Between the father and the five boys we had almost every musical instrument there was, excelling in trombone, piano and violin. Reggie was an excellent violinist, having passed many exams. When playing all together, they played Selections and Grand Marches, but for myself I preferred sacred music. We were a happy, musical family, until the war broke out, when I buried my eldest son, and two got married. It was a big trouble to me when I lost my son at thirty years of age, but it was a bigger trial when I buried my husband eleven months after. And then my other two sons was called out to war, and I was left alone for two years. Just then I thought all my trouble had come, when the four sons had gone to the war, but, thank God, they came back quite safe. Since then I have buried another son and his wife, at thirty years old. I have been a widow fourteen years, and my youngest son is still with me.

Had it not been that I took an interest in public work, I could not have stood it. There was the Women's Co-operative Guild, to which I owe a great deal for my education. I have been a member from the beginning of our Branch, a worker on Committees, and President for two years. We are glad to think that we in the Guild have taken our place in the fight for better conditions for women and children.

I joined the Suffrage, because having had such a hard and difficult life myself, I thought I would do all I could to relieve the sufferings of others. I took great interest in all women's organizations. When the war broke out, I helped on the Relief Committees all through the war. Miss Wilkinson (now M.P.) was one of the first to open a workroom in Stockport, to find work for girls in making old clothes for new for the poor children. We went round begging old cast-offs, and good work was done. Miss Wilkinson helped towards getting the Maternity Centre formed in Stockport. When investigating cases for relief we came across many pitiful homes where father had gone to the war, and four or five children had to be fed.

I don't think we should have had war if the women could have had the vote before, and a voice in it. There's no mother or wife in England nor Germany that would give their loved one to be killed. Now we are working for peace.

I can't say that I have read many books as I have had no time. What I have read has been Guild and Co-operative literature and newspapers, for I have learnt a great deal through newspapers. As far as politics go I am very fond of history. I like to go back to the olden times and to know more of our forefathers, and I get a lot out of my Bible.

I am seventy-two and shall carry on with the Guild as long as I can.

In a Mining Village

By Mrs F. H. Smith

I am not much of a scholar as I had to leave school at an early age owing to my father not being in regular employment. I am a native of Cardiff and went to service up the Rhondda where I had a brother working, and it was there I met my husband, who was a miner. I was nineteen when I married in 1903. As a town-bred girl I found the life very different from what I had been used to. I was very shocked that we had no convenience for our husbands to bath in. We had to bring a tub or tin bath, whichever we had, into the same room that we lived in, and heat the water over our living-room fire in a bucket or iron boiler, whichever we possessed. So you can imagine the life of a miner's wife is no bed of roses. We have also to do our weekly wash in the same room, so our one room was not much to look at. By the time we had done our daily clean, it was looking all right, until Hubby came home.

Then after he had bathed and his clothes put to dry, and turned from time to time, there is a nice film of coal dust all over the room, and it means you want the duster in your hand continually. Well, time went on and eleven months after my marriage my first daughter was born, and as she grew older it was very trying, as no matter how you try to keep your baby nice and clean it is practically impossible.

When she was just a year old I was lucky enough to rent a house under the Colliery Company for which my husband worked, and we had hardly settled down before we had the terrible experience of a pit explosion. My husband was down the pit at the same time, but was working in what they call the New Pit, and the explosion was in the Old Pit. But it will always live in my memory the terrible scenes I witnessed among the men and boys and neighbours from around me. One poor woman opposite me lost her husband, two sons and an adopted son in that terrible blast – lost all her breadwinners. There was only one survivor and 122 killed.

Well, as I said, it was very close quarters in two rooms – one living-room and one bedroom. It was much better to have a house, though it meant more furniture to fill the six rooms now, or partially. As my husband was a steady, sober man we had a chance to get on a bit in that way. In the course of time my family increased until I had nine children, but what is the most tragic thing is, that my husband's health has failed since 1925, he was home ill before the strike of 1926, for seven months after a serious operation for haemorrhoids, and general debility set in after the operation. He has lost time continuously until last year he was home ill with neuritis in the head for nine and a half months. When he got a bit better he went to look for light employment at the pit where he worked last. There was none to be had, so they have put him on the Unemployment List. But, of course, I have not all my children at home, as my eldest girl is now twenty-six and is married and has two children of her own, and like myself she too has married a miner. Next were three boys. I buried two and have one twenty-one in May. He is not at home, but is working on a ship, as he did not like pit work. He was only down for a short time, and before the strike and when I had the chance, I sent him to London as a pantry-boy and from there he has got to a ship. I have five girls now at home, the eldest is seventeen in June. She came home ill with a breakdown in the latter part of last year, and has now obtained a situation. Next come twins aged thirteen, then one nine, and one five, and my husband and myself to keep out of £1 12s. and to pay 7/10 rent out of that. My eldest girl who has been at home did not get anything to keep her as she had not got enough stamps on her Insurance Card.

I honestly think my husband's ill-health and subsequent unemployment is through the rotten conditions we are living and working under. The hours of work in the pit are 7 till 3 p.m., 3 till 11 p.m., 11 till 6 a.m. One cage full of men goes down and another comes up. As to meals, they are allowed twenty minutes for food when they feel it is time and they carry their food in tin boxes, and water is the general thing they take to drink in the pit, carried in tin bottles. Sometimes the part of the pit my husband is working in is very cold, and the last place he was working in was terribly hot, and he had to take an extra singlet and trousers to work every day, as he could not work in the same clothes in which he went back and fore to work. By the time he has finished his day's work he has not a dry thread on him. So just imagine him bringing his pit clothes home, and we wives have to wash the singlet every night and dry the trousers, and by the time the trousers is dry they are stiff with perspiration and coal dust. The houses here are not built for the convenience of the tenant, as we have no baths where they are most needed. As you know the miner has to bath every day. They are at present building some pit-head baths in Wallstown, but whether they will be favoured I cannot say. The majority of the miners are ready for their food when they come home from the pit. They just wash their hands and sit down to their food and perhaps a smoke, and sometimes a nap if they are very tired. So you see, to go straight to bath, it would be something very different. Some live a long way from the pit and have either to walk or take a tram.

Also we have no boilers, or coppers I should say, to boil our clothes in. We have to boil them over the living-room fire. No wonder so many little children are scalded to death in Wales, as many people, unthinking, put the hot water in the bath first, forgetful of the little ones toddling around them, and they stumble into it. A little one, living close by me, five years old, died last week through falling in a bath of boiling water that was being prepared for his father to bath. So you see how much we need baths in our homes. In our village we have nothing for recreation, except a Picture Palace, the British Legion (men's and women's sections), and unfinished playing fields. The fields could not be finished owing to lack of funds. I am living between two idle collieries, that were working full time before the 1926 lock-out, and it makes a lot of difference to the local funds, because as a rule each miner contributes so much per week to such things, but now they are not working that is out of the question. The Society of Friends in the next village has given a good sum of money to be distributed through the valleys for this purpose, but it is not enough. It is a great pity as they only employed men and boys who had no relief of any kind. So it was really doing two-fold good. But there are two lovely Parks, with paddling pools, swings and the usual things for children, within walking distance of us, namely Porth Park and Wattstown Park. Also there are lovely mountain walks where we send the children when it is nice weather, and in the summer we picnic *en* family, as we never go away only to the Sunday School outing, which is to Barry Island or Porthcawl. I can honestly say I have not otherwise had a holiday since I married.

In this part of the country the houses are built all along the mountain-sides. There are ninety-six houses in the row which you can see from my back-garden.

I wish it were possible for you to come amongst us without anyone knowing of your presence, as you would understand better by seeing than hearsay. It is heartbreaking to see the unemployed miners at the Labour

Exchange – boys, young men in their prime and old men, idle owing to the pits being shut down. The women most steadily support their men in their Trade Unions. And let me tell you what it is that keeps me from getting despondent many a time. I have found out, and I wish that many other wives and mothers could see the same as I have done, that the Co-operative Stores is a great boon to help those who cannot help themselves, and also the Women's Co-operative Guild is a great help, and I would not miss going for anything, as we have such very beautiful lectures from our different speakers that it seems to uplift us and help us to carry on from time to time. We feel sometimes that we are not living but just existing somehow.

A Guild Office Clerk

Contributed by the Editor

An exceptional woman – Harriet A. Kidd – worked in the Guild Office from 1906 to 1917, when she died. Of an unusually strong and courageous character, with great force of will, she never spared herself in battling for the rights of women and labour. She attacked unflinchingly the views she held wrong. Outspoken, ready for an argument with anyone, she would always win respect by her sincerity. How angry she was with what she felt was sham or self-seeking or pretentious in individuals, and how resentful that the workers did not share in all the advantages of the rich! With so uncompromising and independent a nature, combined with a hard and difficult life, she was not an easy person to live or work with. She was jealous of anyone who might come between herself and her friends or work, and an imagined slight of any kind would fill the atmosphere with an overpowering gloom and silence. Many of her characteristics might be traced in relatives on both her father's and mother's side. Two persons of whom she used to talk, stood out prominently. Her grandfather was a Fenian who had to leave Ireland because of his politics, 'a dear delightful old Irish gentleman' and a Catholic. On the other side was a remarkable grandmother. Miss Kidd related that 'Mother' as she always called her, was carried to the mill at three years old, and set on a stool to turn a handle for the same number of hours as any adult. This astonishing woman never went to school, and taught herself to read at sixty. She was a great democrat and followed closely the politics of the day. She left work at seventy-three, but could not rest, and returned to the mill where she worked till a few months before her death at eighty-three. In eighty years she had only left the mill at the periods when her twelve children were born.

Miss Kidd herself started work in a Silk Mill at Leek (Staffs) when she was ten years old. As a 'skeiner' her work was to separate and twist up the skeins from the 'bond.' Later she was a 'marker' in the dye-house, that is, one who ties cottons round the 'bonds' to indicate the different quantities and colours needed. In the opinion of the dyers 'there wasn't a better marker on earth.' 'They used,' she said, 'to go on and start an argument and get her in a temper, so that she would go faster, taking it out of her work.' She told me of the different sort of life there was in the mill in those days. Whole families were employed there, and a sort of fatherly relation existed between the employer and workers. The master would augment the wretched wages by paying the school pence of the children or the expense of a funeral. He also felt responsible for the souls of his 'hands.' On Sunday morning he would round up the men standing at street corners, drive them into Church, and seat them all under his eye in his own pew. 'I'll have no street loiterers,' he used to say. The factory was then ill-built and planned, and the girls were much at the mercy of the employers. She said how much things had changed since those days, the workers being more independent, and the buildings far better arranged, though the strain of the work had increased.

When a mill-worker, Miss Kidd became a member of the Leek Co-operative Society, and as her card of membership showed, she joined the Leek Branch of the Guild in 1897. She was Secretary of her Branch, and also of the Macclesfield District. Regardless, even reckless, of her health, she 'sat up all hours of the night doing writing work for the Guild.' Or, after evening meetings in the

District, she would go straight to the mill in the early morning without going to bed. She also became an ardent propagandist of Trade Unionism among the mill girls. She helped to start the Union, and she became the first President, and in a short time the membership reached 2,000. She also stood as a Poor Law Guardian, and though unsuccessful received 484 votes, a remarkable poll for the time and place, when public opinion thought women 'ought to have enough work to do at home.'

She was earning 12/6 as a 'marker' in 1906, when a letter reached her, giving her, she felt, the great opportunity of her life. It asked her to come as a clerk into the Guild Office, which was then at Kirkby Lonsdale, Westmorland. In her reply she wrote as follows: 'The writing of this letter is one of, nay, it *is*, the hardest task I have ever been called on to perform during the whole of my life. I had hoped someone would have informed you of the story of my past, but I fear such is not the case. Many times I have wondered if it was possible to tell you of it without your knowing I was the one concerned, but I shrank from it fearing your condemnation. Now I must tell you, painful though it may be. Do not judge me too harshly when I tell you that I have been a mother for twenty-two years. When I was a girl of seventeen my then employer, a gentleman of good position and high standing in the town, sent me to his home one night, ostensibly to take a parcel of books, but really with a very different object. When I arrived at the house all the family were away, and before he would allow me to leave he forced me to yield to him. At eighteen I was a mother. During the first years of my boy's life my employer compelled me by threats to keep the knowledge of his part in the affair a secret, and I had to bear the whole of the burden myself. My people, who were also in his employ, suspected him but did not dare to charge him, consequently the real truth never transpired. Through the whole of my life since, I have never done anything of which any man or woman could point a finger at me. I have never accepted any position in my own town only at the oft-expressed wish of those with whom I have worked, and they have known me all my life.'

Such an incident was not one to stand in the way of her appointment as clerk in the Guild Office, and only rendered more striking the position she had won in her own town. This event undoubtedly cast a shadow over her life, but she had real happiness in the mutual love which existed between mother and son.

She became gradually more and more absorbed into the

life of the Guild and into the warm friendship of Guild members. While at the office in Kirkby Lonsdale, she underwent a severe operation at Liverpool, from which she did not make a good recovery. In 1908 she migrated with the Guild Office to Hampstead, where she shared a small flat, in which she delighted, with a Guild friend.

It is not too much to say that she lived for the Guild. After nine years she was attacked by a fatal illness. 'Eh, the dear old Guild,' she exclaimed one day when I was sitting by her bed, 'it has been a good friend to me.' Another day she said, 'There's a pound or two in the Store. I want the Guild to have it. I should love it. I'd forgot all about it.' And I found that years ago she said she desired her A.U.C.E. burial money to go to the Guild, having been also insured in another Club at Leek.

In the Guild Office she became an excellent typist. She had an instinct for machinery, and the instrument behaved better with her than with anyone else, and she did not like any others to work on it. At her bedside, a few weeks before she died, I had some typewritten papers in my hands, and she looked and said, 'Oh, what a shame! I see my little machine I'm sure.' Although she had had so little in the way of education, she had been a great reader and writer, often after her work at the mill spending the whole night reading in bed. She had a very good vocabulary, and her spelling was practically never at fault.

She was also our Cashier, and kept the Guild accounts. She would stay behind in the office many hours beyond closing time, doing up her books, because she then had quiet and 'all the tables to herself.' When the Central Committee met, or when Guild 'Schools' were held at the office, she would be caterer and cook and deal out lunches and teas and suppers. And at the end of these days, she used to carry off the members to her flat for the night, 'where sympathy and love grew and flourished.' As one of them said, 'Remembrance of the fun and the discussions on these occasions will remain with all those who crowded into her small rooms.'

An active worker in the A.U.C.E. (Amalgamated Union of Co-operative Employees), she was the first women to be elected to an official position in the Union. A fellow Guildswoman said of her: 'She was a great advocate of the right of women to direct their own lives, to have the vote, and to receive equal pay for their work, and she fought for her belief in many an industrial and political battle.'

It might be said that the only recreations she gave herself, except the theatre, where she was an enthusiastic admirer of Gerald du Maurier, were Hyde Park and Trafalgar Square meetings. She was brought up as a Wesleyan Methodist, but under the influence of Socialists at Leek, she wholeheartedly adopted the Socialist faith, and made her religion one with the cause of the people. For some time she was caretaker at the William Morris Labour Church (an old Quaker Church, decorated by Larner Sugden, the Socialist architect), where she heard addresses from all the prominent Socialists. Her favourite song was the 'Red Flag,' and her hero, Keir Hardie. In London, she sometimes went to the Friends' Meeting House, nearly opposite her flat, where the kindly and democratic atmosphere suited her nature; but she said that 'amongst the refined ladies there she felt like a bull in a china shop.'

It was in July, 1916, that the terrible shock of her fatal illness came. In spite of suffering and growing weakness, she came off and on to the Office and attended A.U.C.E. and other meetings till Easter. The Fund so willingly contributed by the Guild enabled her to have what care nurses could give her, while visits from her Leek and Guild friends brought the mental consolation which was so much more to her than physical comfort.

Her funeral at the Golders Green Crematorium took place on July 10th, 1917.

A Felt Hat Worker

By Mrs Scott, J.P.

My first clear recollection is of the time when I was about three years of age, when we lived near a hollow where a little girl had been maltreated and killed by a gang of youths. Mother told me I was not to go down to the hollow, because it was not safe for little girls. I remember getting something to drag behind me and asking one or two more children to venture with me, and going down to the hollow to see if anything really did happen to you. Although it is so long ago, I can still feel the thrill of marching down and seeing for myself. This I suppose was the beginning of my habit of testing things for myself and not taking facts and opinions ready-made. Of course, that is one of the great things in our Guild Movement, placing the facts before our members, and letting them judge for themselves whether to accept or reject.

My father was a man who never made money at the

expense of other people, and only his own family suffered. He could have made sure of a portion of the fortune of the ladies who employed him after his master's death, if only he would have turned Conservative and Church, but he stood to his Liberalism. I was pleased the other day when I was ill, and one of our Guild members brought me the most lovely flowers because my father was good to her when she was a child, and found her her first situation. It comforted me and helped me to forget.

When I was seven years old we went to keep a draper's shop and we were in business for eleven years. I think those years have bred in me a horror of debt, for every Christmas there were rates, promissory notes, etc., falling due. Neither father nor mother had a business mind, they were not keen on people in debt, and I had to go round collecting on Saturday afternoons, and how I did hate it! Then, although only a child, I heard of the club system and people getting 'fast,' certain dealers letting young girls have all sorts of finery until they were deep in debt.

My father and mother always took a keen interest in politics, also my grandparents on father's side. Grandfather was a real old Tory, grandmother a Liberal, both of old Derbyshire families. Then mother's father was one of the men who came to Stockport when the Plug

Riots were on. He used to tell of coming with his knee breeches, blue stockings and blue neckerchief, from Holcombe in Lancashire with blankets and provisions. They were stopped at Stockport, where he settled down. His aunt lived with him, and when I was a little girl, I used to sit and listen to her telling of their little mill at Windsor, how her father used to start off with the family, two born at Windsor, one at Bray and others in Lancashire. Two of her brothers were press-ganged; she used to say they came home, one lamed and the other blind, with their faces painted and their hair tied up. She was ninety-five when she died and has been dead forty-five years. Then one of our visitors was a Bradlaughite, and we children used to look at him with awe because he was an atheist. I can see him now, with blue eyes just like pin points, so sharp and clear. And the arguments there used to be! I was only very small, very fond of reading, and I could get under the counter with my book and hear all the talk, or sit in the corner of the fender; and even though I had my book all these talks were a great joy to me. Mother was a strict Congregationalist, but she went to hear Charles Bradlaugh and Annie Besant; also Enid Stacey when she came. Then it all had to be talked over and the impressions received, so that though only a child

I was learning and was allowed to speak. Mother used to call me little Lydia Becker. I always remember her going across to my uncle's, who was deeply interested in Darwin, Ruskin, William Morris and all other leaders of advanced thought of fifty years ago, and coming back home saying, 'Poor Alfred is talking some nonsense about the survival of the fittest and the weakest going to the wall,' and every night for some time afterwards, mother trudged across with her knitting to argue the case for the weak. This uncle was a great reader and used to read aloud so that we knew and loved the characters in Dickens' works. Also he attended all the lectures on advanced thought, and I used to go and listen about William Morris, Bradlaugh and Annie Besant, while at home we had *Chambers' Miscellany* and *Chambers' Journals*. I used to sit for hours lost in these books, and Wednesday was a joyful day for it brought *The Family Circle* and *The Girls' Own Paper*. I used to creep downstairs to see if they were under the shop door, so that we could read them before we went to school. We went through the usual girls' books, *The Wide Wide World*, *Queechy*, *The Lamplighter*, and at our Sunday School we had a very good library, where the librarian used to let me roam through the shelves. One book from there made me keen on housing and garden cities. It was *The Door without a Knocker*, deeply religious, but one conversation between husband and wife has always influenced me. The husband told the wife if she built a town, it would be all baths, kitchens and washhouses, and she retorted that if he built one, it would be all art galleries, museums and parks. I wondered why they could not be combined, and I have sat hours at work planning a city, fitting in beautiful homes and everything to make life beautiful and happy, instead of sordid and ugly like our factory towns. I always remember going down a street lined with great mills on either side and hoping I should never have to bring a child into the world if it was condemned to that life, for I reasoned: If I were asked to work in one of these mills (for I do not like machinery) I should hate it, and I have no right to bring anyone else if this is all we can offer it, because I should love it too much to give it such a life. And when I read that wonderful chapter in *The Blue Bird* where the unborn babies are waiting for their mothers, it strengthened that feeling.

When I was twelve I went to work in the hat shops. We sat on a little wooden block in the passage between the tables and behind our 'Missus,' who sat at the table on a higher stool or chair. There we sat, lashing in the leathers. We were not allowed to speak unless we were spoken to, and not supposed to laugh at any joke we heard. Fortunately they were a decent set of girls, and in that room at any rate the lashers were safe from all kind of loose talk; but this particular kind of work was dispensed with, and soon afterwards I went to work amongst an entirely different set of girls who were much older than I was, and, though I did not know it then, were prostitutes. I was only fourteen. We had to be at work at 6.20 a.m., and the works were over a mile from home. There was the compensation of seeing the day break, and we had to pass some beautiful trees, but on cold, frosty mornings, road like glass, afraid of being one minute late, there was not very much pleasure in work. Then the room, one big room, was warehouse, machine room and trimming room, half taken up with six tables. Ten people sat at each, mounted on three-legged stools, gas lights on a level with the eyes, steam, and ventilation only up the staircase, with hundreds of dozens of hats in the room. It was terrible, and the girls I worked with were not particular about morals. They were fast. Fortunately I did not understand all, but used to think they had some good times. And still this always puzzled me: they worked hard, got good wages, and you heard of the presents they received but they never had any money for holidays and could not even pay their way. And they used to tell some awful stories of the girls who were kept in the houses in Manchester, having no clothes only the ones that belonged to the proprietress, and how unhappy they were. I suppose I must have amused them, for I found out they knew very little of history and geography, so we used to learn the capitals of Europe and Asia and have lessons, etc., and I used to write their love letters for them. But there were some girls who worked there, members of the G.F.S., who took an interest in real things, so I found some friends there.

I was living with my uncle at this time; he was a traveller in America and Canada, and used to bring home magazines and books. He brought Bellamy's *Looking Backward* – that was a revelation, something to live for – *John Ward, Preacher, Robert Elsmere* and others. How I used to enjoy the American papers, and I have never lost my love of *Harper's, The Century,* and *Scribner's*. But at this time I had a serious illness, was in bed for three months, and if I had not been at uncle's with everything provided I should have died. I remember one night I was very ill, and they brought in someone, and I had heard she had a reputation for snatching pillows from under people's heads if they were near death. I thought if she tries to do that, I will try to hold her, but she did not do that but put a scalding poultice on me.

When I got better, I went to work at Christie's Hat Works in a lovely room, six stories up, with big windows and a splendid view of the hills. We had to be at work by 7 a.m., and you could see the day break over the hills, and they are always such a comfort and help. In spite of very hard work I always look back with pleasure to that room, and we had some good times. There were some good old Tories at my table, and we had such times! One said that they sat round the fire and thanked God they had all married Conservatives. She did not speak to me for three months because I said that the charwoman who had brought her family up and kept them respectable was as much to be admired as Queen Victoria. If you could have seen the look of her face and heard the bated breath which she said, 'But she kept herself pure!' Still I think that even she votes Labour now, for I met her last year and she said that all I told her years ago she had found to be true.

I had loved working at Christie's because of the work-room, but the hats were very hard. If your wrist was not very strong you could not push the needle through or pull it out. Then, in the room I was in, there were several who worked for 'honour,' priding themselves in never putting a crooked stitch in their work, in fact giving their lives to their work. When they were put on to look over our work it was terrible. Just think of the binding on men's hat brims; if they were a quarter of an inch or even less crooked, back they came, and you had to take them off and do them over again. And the fine leathers – a crooked stitch in those, and you had to take them out. One of the old trimmers was terrible with me; she said it was for my good she wanted to make a perfect trimmer of me, but I could not see it. We were working hard all day, bringing work home and working until eight or nine o'clock at nights for 13/- or 15/- per week, so I left and went to work at Lees and Hatconk's. I wish you could have seen that workroom. It had been built for a warehouse, thick glass windows and a tank of water on the roof which leaked. The room was low, and when the lights were lit it was awful, damp streaming down the walls. Still we had some good times. I worked with a Conservative, an Irish girl, and some Radicals and Socialists, and we used to have full dress debates. When we began someone would call 'Parliament is now sitting' (this is thirty years ago), and we would discuss everything.

I remember once, after I was married, the Irish girl came one Monday and said: 'Nellie, the priest said last night all married people who had no children would go to hell,' and I retorted: 'I should think I deserved to go to hell if I had brought some of the children into the world I have seen.'

At this time we had joined the Clarion Fellowship, and there was a Ruskin Hall Settlement in Stockport which we had joined, and it was a treat to go on the rambles studying botany, geology, economics, etc., there was real comradeship. I met Mr Scott at a Cinderella treat; we were both kneeling melting butter for the tea and got talking afterwards. We had to forgo a Committee meeting so we could have a walk together, and I think most of our courtship was spent in giving tickets out, going to Committee meetings, etc. Still we kept on, and I determined to make the plunge of getting married. He was getting 22/- a week and we had to give a small sum to his mother. My wages did not amount to much more than 10/- per week and there were my people to think of. We had £20 for furniture, and enough to pay for a week's honeymoon and wedding. I said it was like diving in cold water, but we did it. We had our week; we did not know where we were going until we were on the station, but found ourselves in North Wales. And we have pulled through though times have been very dark sometimes. Still in the early days of the Labour Church, although I was going out to work, there was always hospitality for any comrade.

It was whilst at Lees' that I joined the Felt Hatters' Trade Union. They had tried to organize the trimmers very often; all the men were in the Union but only about six of the trimmers. Well, I joined, also a friend of mine. Then we began to try to get the other girls in. It was hard work, the answer would be, 'I will when the others do.' So one day we went round with a list (there had been a lot of trouble over the work) and said, 'Just put your name down, those who will join if the others will consent,' and behold, we got the majority. We called a meeting, and in the meantime I had seen the men and told them they ought not to consider working with non-unionists, so they sent up a note saying they would not consent to work any longer with non-unionist trimmers, and after some persuasion, every trimmer joined the Union. Of course, the men at other shops tried to get their trimmers in, but they were more obstinate than ours so the masters locked us out for six weeks. It was a time; my sister was out, there was father, auntie, my sister and baby, and the income was only 11/- per week; but we got through. Then when we got back to work there was some further trouble and we had a stay-in strike. After it was settled I went down for my work, and the fore-mistress said, 'I am sorry, Nellie, but I cannot serve you.' I went back and told the girls, and everyone put down their work and two of those who had been worst against the Union went down to see the head of the firm. They all sat there until I was sent for and told it was a mistake. I always feel proud of the way they all stood by me.

It was whilst at this work that mother died before I was married, and I joined the Cooperative Society. Mother had been the member and when she died I went down to have the book transferred to me. They asked if I had a father. I said, 'Yes,' so they told me he would have to become the member or I must get his consent. I stood and looked at them, then said, 'My father takes no interest in this or in anything concerning us, and if I am not made the member not one penny will be spent here.' But they made me the member right away and I still have the same number we have had for over forty years. At our work we had many debates over Co-operation, and one thing always struck me; it was the poorest people in the room that were the most loyal. Ideals had nothing to do with it, it was the 'divi.' that was so useful. We had members of three Societies working and it was wonderful how keen they were over the Stores, mainly for saving purposes. I was gradually becoming drawn into the Labour Movement and was treasurer of the Women's Labour League, on the Labour Representation Committee, Clarion Fellowship and Cinderella. Then in our work we had to bring work home, sometimes sitting up until twelve o'clock making linings. When we joined the Union that was one of the first things stopped. Even then you could not make the girls see that we ought to earn a decent wage without working meal times and taking work home; it was a hard struggle, but it was stopped and we had the nights to ourselves, though in those days there was housework to be done, baking at night and cleaning, but my auntie was very good and used to help me very much.

Reading has always been a great pleasure to me, and I never remember learning to read, but when I was a little girl I used to sit for hours with a great *Chambers' Journal* propped up before me. I love J. M. Barrie's books; one laughs and cries, and feels with Grizel that one can sit and rock and hold oneself tight with sheer delight. His books are wonderful and his plays. I do feel silly, but I sit with tears running down at *Peter Pan* and *Mary Rose* – that sense of longing and stretching out after dreams and ideals is so vivid. Then, of course, George Eliot's books, and Charles Kingsley – I have read all his, *Hypatia* many times. Then one of George Egerton's is a special treasure, *Rosa Amorosa*, a series of such delightful love letters; I only lend that to special friends. H. G. Wells – how one revels in *Kipps*. I can sympathise with him in some of his situations when one is not used to hotels, etc. I did feel pleased when he put a shilling in the musical box, and left them all gasping. 'Mr Polly' – what a delight he is, and in *The Dream* how Wells hits off the class we belong to, the small shopkeepers, etc. We have been reading *William Clissold*, but it needs careful reading and study; it is a wonderful book. There is always one thing about Wells' books – you seem to know the characters and he has an uncanny knowledge of funeral parties, etc., and the conversations carried on at such gatherings by some of the older women. He must have been a quiet listener and a keen observer as a child. When I was about sixteen I was very fond of George Macdonald's books and they influenced my views on religion – David Elginbrod with his epitaph:

'Hae mercy on me Lord God,
As I would do if I were God
And thou wast David Elginbrod,'

and *Robert Falconer*. That is a splendid book, the grand-mother is such a fine character, just like some of our old chapel people. My mother and my grandfather were of that type.

Then we get into different company with *Looking Backward*, which I read when it was first published; I felt as though my dream city was coming true. When we joined the Clarion Fellowship we attended classes on Botany and Geology and found

'Sermons in stones
Books in the running brooks
And good in everything.'

and we truly read 'The Manuscripts of God.' I had always loved stones and pebbles and now they were a story book that we could read, and the country was full of new delight.

I have read Colonel Repington's diary, and advised all our members to read it to teach them, if possible, how the people are regarded merely as pawns in a game and how the war-makers made war lightly, and callously regarded the loss of life. I also read Wilfrid Blunt's diary. These books should be read by the workers because they find a different point of view and how we are thought of by the other class.

Pelle the Conqueror and *Ditte Girl Alive*, by Nexo, a Danish writer, are wonderful books, though they make your flesh creep with the sordid pictures of the life of the poor in Denmark. Pelle found his salvation through Co-operation. I have been reading Floyd Dell's books, they are good, and Sinclair Lewis – I have read all with the exception of the last book. Babbitt, how you meet him every day going down to business. Mr Wrenn, we sat and chuckled over him, for if there is one special weakness we have it is maps, railway guides and guide books. I come home with books of tours, Norway, Sweden, trips up the Nile and to Italy, and I daresay we know more of these places than some who visit them, so when we found a kindred spirit in Mr Wrenn, we were quite pleased. I like the American novels and magazines. We can get them out of our library which is very up-to-date.

When I am ill I read all my old favourites over again, Dickens, Thackeray, these are always new, and if I want nature, we have all the works of Richard Jeffries, and in poetry, we have Browning, Lowell, Longfellow, Tennyson, Whittier and Shakespeare. We can read them and

> 'The cares that infest the day
> Fold their tents like the Arabs
> And silently steal away.'

It was in 1907 that it was suggested to me that we form a Women's Co-operative Guild in Stockport, and would I be the Secretary. Mr Perry was the President of our Society, and as I never missed a meeting, I suppose he thought I was interested. It was in 1908 and I promised to try. We had a big tea-party and the Guild was formed, and a new world was opened with new opportunities of service and knowledge. With our three Guilds we have nearly 300 members in our Society, and hope to increase these shortly when I can get to Cheadle, Hulme and Bramhall. When the Guild was formed there was not a woman in any position, but now we have six women delegates to the Co-operative Wholesale Society, four scrutineers, two on the Management Committee and three on the Educational Committee. I was the first woman delegate to the C.W.S., first members' delegate to Conferences and Congress, and was delegate to the International Conference. When a woman stood for any position in those days the abuse they met with was awful. I stood for Management Committee, and my husband and the wife of the man who proposed me had some dreadful postcards sent to them. Now women take their place alongside the men, but there still remains much to be done. I think, sometimes, when I hear the women speaking of the influence of the Guild, what a wonderful organization it is, and what it has meant to so many women.

I left the hat works for a place as superintendent at a Centre for feeding school children and was there four years, a most strenuous time during the first year of the war when we had nearly 300 children each day at our Centre. From there I went to be sickness visitor for an Approved Society. My district was in Derbyshire, thirty miles one way by fifteen the other – Hayfield and the Moors round Buxton, Chapel-en-le-Frith down back to Stockport. I had this for seven years, including all the war period except the first year. I have walked fifteen or twenty miles a day, tramping over the hills and the dales, visiting farms and houses miles apart. The train service was very bad, and there were no fires in the waiting-rooms and no places to get meals.

But how I loved the country!* I used to take a book with me and I was never lonely and never afraid. I was on Chinley Churn one day, nearly 2,000 feet up, crouched on the hillside during a thunderstorm. I have been over the hilltops when the snowdrifts were over three feet high, and six feet in some places. I was in a blizzard in Hayfield and thought I should never get round the corners. But it was life on the moors; I seemed to know every blade of grass and where the flowers grew, and all the little streams were my companions. In those days you would walk miles and never meet anyone. Then, in the homes I was made welcome, always a little chat and often a cup of tea – people were very kind. But the life was just a bit too strenuous along with all my other work and home worries, and one day the doctor came when I was ill; then came a special examination, and the doctor told me I had strained my heart and might live for some time

---

*Another Guildswoman, writing as follows, shows her love of nature: 'Oh! Work it is a blessed thing! Give me lots of it! I got up at 5.30 this a.m. to go to a case. The world was one casket of glittering gems, the moon was as bright as gold, the roofs and roads were white and sparkling with frost – all was peaceful and still. The case was a B.B. one, drat it! It was a *boy*, too! However all was well, but I do hate the baby to arrive before me – it is not cricket.'

if I went quietly or might die any time. No more hills. I was alone in the house and it was a shock. But there it was, and I had had those years of beauty, seeing nature in all her moods, roaming over the hilltops, meeting people, giving the message in the homes of the people, trying to sow the seeds of Co-operation and fellowship all during the war. So I felt that stage is done and you must do your best with what is left, and my favourite thought came to me:

'Machinery just meant
To give thyself its bent
Try thee and turn thee forth sufficiently impressed.'

The people were all sorry when I told them for I had been able to do many little kindnesses for them through being on the Pensions' Committee and Insurance Committee; so many are robbed of benefits and pensions through ignorance.

I find my work as a magistrate very interesting. I had an experience not long ago. The Chief Constable came in and said there was a very unpleasant case – a man applying for a warrant against another man on a charge of indecency – and if any magistrate wished to go they were at liberty to do so. Then he said, if Mrs Scott does not wish to hear the case, she can go. So I asked if it was the case of a woman applying, would the men go? At once they said no. Then he said if Mrs Scott likes to stop, of course she can. I was vexed and I said, Mrs Scott does not *like* to hear unpleasant cases, but I was appointed a magistrate to hear all cases, and I consider it my duty to take the unpleasant ones along with the others. If it is a rule for the men to try a woman, then I consider I am only doing the right thing, and I shall stop. I told them if I had heard of a woman magistrate leaving the bench I should not consider her fit to fill the position. Anyway, they will not trouble again, but it is not an easy thing to face the surprised looks, but I think they thought it over and it was all right.

When I look back and think of the Labour Church (I was on the national executive), how we tried to make it a real living force and thought we had failed, and yet we come across evidence of the good work done by the Movement and all the other Movements, Women's Suffrage, Internationalism and many others, we find the seed has brought forth fruit, not always in the way we thought but still it is there. I think if you begin right and keep straight on, following the principles laid down in the Guild, even if we may lose a few members, eventually we shall regain our position. During the war we kept firm in our opposition to war and worked for peace. Our membership fell from over 100 to about 20, 12 attending our meetings sometimes. But to-day we have 150 members with an average attendance of nearly 100. The men look on and think it is wonderful how we get the numbers and keep up the interest, but we are not satisfied yet and if we could get more rooms we should start branches in outlying districts. There are thousands of Guildswomen who have given of their best ungrudgingly with no hope of material gain, but only the thoughts of making the path a little easier for those who follow. I feel ashamed sometimes when I think of some of our women, how they have worked and striven, for truly the life of a working-woman with a large family is one of constant self-denial. It is always a joy to hear how the Guild has helped several who have been through deep trouble. They have told me that if it had not been for the Guild they would have gone right under, but it has given them strength and courage to fight their battle. Of such is the fellowship formed which is true and lasting. One of our members is out in India, her husband managing a cotton mill. They had some deep trouble before they went, but she said it was worth the suffering for the friendship she had met in the Guild. And out in India she is trying to put the ideals into practice, going in to the crèche at the mill where there are seventy babies. She got the place cleaned and whitewashed, and she goes down each morning to wash the babies, attend to their sores and teach the mothers how to attend to them. I thought it was just lovely of her, and she said she just sat on the verandah looking at the stars sending a message to her Guild sisters in England and feeling grateful for the knowledge she had gained of fellowship with all, whether black or white. During the war she was one of the keenest in her belief in the war; she was quite willing that her sons should go and proud one had died. She often said how hard she was when first she came to our meetings, but quite different before she left. We also had a Frenchwoman, and after hearing a pacifist giving a lecture on a visit to Germany, well, she was frantic, saying 'Canaille,' but when we asked for gifts for the German women and children sometime afterwards, she was the first to bring a gift. I was pleased, especially when she said she looked at things differently now. She was in Amiens all the war time, and her people are still there. So we can always look back and feel, though despondent sometimes, still 'it moves,' if slowly yet surely towards the better time. When we think of the great and noble women who have made the path, like the story in Olive Schreiner's *Dreams*, by giving their lives and thoughts to making it easy for those who follow, we cannot feel too much or speak too highly of those who founded our Movement, the Women's Co-operative Guild, which has meant so much to the working-woman, brought new visions and opened the doors and windows so that we may see the City Beautiful. Also it taught us to become articulate and able to ask for the things we need. For so many, although they have known the needs and desired a better system of society, have not been able to express themselves. But I do think that, in the coming years, with the greater freedom given to women, and also the vote (the key to open so many doors), we shall reap the harvest of the years of sowing the good seed.

A Public-Spirited Rebel

By Mrs Yearn

Some memories of my childhood days are not of the best. We had a very large family – fourteen children – eight of them laid in ground at a very early age, six of us left, and too many even then to feed and clothe. I can well remember having to stay at home to look after mother when two of the younger children were born. I can picture her now having the mug brought to the bedside, so to be able to wash out little things that were required. Thank goodness, such conditions don't obtain to-day.

My father was a brick-setter by trade, and you will realise fifty years ago what that meant. We had the terrible winters of frost and snow, and for six or seven months in the year father was unable to work, so mother had to go to the mill, leaving us in the frail hands of an elder sister. My job was to take the baby into the mill to be fed twice a day. Eventually things became a little better. We had grown up, and as one became full-time, another was ready to be half-time. Mother joined the Stores. How well I remember going with her and carrying the flour tied up in a check handkerchief on my head. And when Whitsuntide came round, we were the first out showing our new clothes. So proud were we of them. They were the first we had made by a dressmaker. Sorry indeed to say my mother died from cancer, just when we were able to give her the best.

I got married, and yet fate seemed to dog my life. In the first year my husband was out of work nine months, through the Engineers' strike. After the second baby I went to work again – at the same mill as the Right Honourable J. R. Clynes used to work at when he was quite a boy. What a time I had there! Being a Trade Unionist I expected they all were, but when the manager found out, he did all he could to make me uncomfortable. Yet I worked there for two years, and during that time I had got nearly all the women to be members of the Trade Union. The legacy left to me for that was the sack.

It was then I joined the Women's Co-operative Guild. Being a little nosey, I was not long before being elected on the Committee. My first Congress to attend was at Liverpool in 1915, when the half-time question came to the front. That made me a real rebel, and helped me to work wholeheartedly for a better state of existence.

I may claim to be the pioneer of women in Oldham as far as Co-operative and Labour women are concerned, and I had many a rough word. When I was a candidate for the Town Council I made a personal canvass of the outskirts among the farms. Ned oth' Tum were the first I came to. Perhaps I had better describe this name first. If the father was called Tom Brown and he had a son called Ned, he would be to the native Ned oth' Tum, or if he had a daughter Sarah, she would be Sally oth' Tum. I had no sooner arrived at the door when Ned oth' Turn came out and said, 'Wet does want here?' I told him I was a candidate for the Council and I should be pleased indeed if he would consider me as a likely person to look after his interest. In answer he said, 'Well, I connot believe my own e'en. I dunno what wourl comming to. If tha dunna go whoam I lay this stick across tha back. My interest! If that's edication, no barn of mine 'ill come to that pitch ill tell thee. Thee looking after ous! Whey, little uns who never had a fayther has more whit than tha as.'

The following is a record of my work done since entering the Guild Movement:

1924. Elected a Director of the Oldham Equitable Co-operative Society – the first and only woman to date, of any Society in the District.

1925. First working-woman candidate for Oldham Poor Law Guardians. I was also a candidate for the Town Council, and failed by a small number.

1927. Made a member of Court of Referees, Oldham Unemployment Exchange.

1928. Made a member of Oldham National Health Insurance Committee. Also made a Justice of the Peace for Oldham Borough.

Assisted in forming a Maternity and Child Welfare Centre, now making splendid progress. Served on the Local Committee of the N.S.P.C.C. Served on the Tenants' Defence League – the only woman.

I gained honours for services rendered on behalf of the Sick and Wounded during the War. I received an illuminated address from Dame Sarah Lees, O.B.E., and also a Certificate of Merit from the British Red Cross and the Order of St. John's.

I have the best husband in the world. He allowed me to leave my home many times without a grumble. He is a great believer in women, and says, given their opportunity, things will soon right themselves. Mr Yearn and myself are in excellent health; working for others makes you fit.

On taking up the *Guardian* one morning in 1919, I found Lady Beaverbrook was the talked-of candidate for the vacancy for Ashton-under-Lyne. And I asked myself, are we as a great Co-operative body of women going to stand by and see these things done, when we have such splendid women in our Movement, who have done more noble work in the social reforms for their country, than ever these *Ladies* will ever attempt to do? I thought we should get all our Guilds and Trade Unions, in one united effort, to get one of our women ready. If we are not alive and alert, we shall see the House of Commons filled with these Peeresses. We've had enough of their husbands. Let us put sensible men and women there, if we are to have our own interests looked after.

We have a very good library at our Cooperative Society, and we are able to get some very useful books, which are so helpful to us who have to be Missionaries for the Co-operative Movement.

What I read myself are all the Co-operative papers, that wonderful little book, *Working Men Co-operators*, *Storekeeping Understood*, by Sydney R. Elliott; *Education and Citizenship*, by G. M. Mactavish; *Nationality*, by S. Herbert; *The Municipal Year Book*, *The Local Government Tear Book*, *The History of Old Peru*, *The Voice of the People*, by G. L. Stocks; *Progress and Poverty*, by Henry George; *The Old Nobility*, by Howard Evans; *The Book on Natural Laws*, by William Whitworth, and the *Daily Herald*.

A short time ago I went through a class with Professor Hall at Holyoake House, on 'The Mechanism of Exchange,' dealing with *Currency, Banking and Trade in Peace and War*, by John A. Todd.

My husband reads the same books, with an addition of light reading, and enjoys books by E. Phillips Oppenheim – *The Mischief Maker*, *Stolen Idol*, *The Little Gentleman*, and others.

It has always been my ambition to travel, and the more I read the greater the longing. The International Co-operative Women's Guild is the linking up of true friendship, a real understanding with other countries. That will prevent wars. I speak on the International Guild at our Lancashire Branches, and I think the *Woman's Outlook* is playing a splendid part in bringing the women's work in other nations so much to the front. I find it makes it much easier to talk of peace to the average person. And the Workers' Travel Association has helped a great deal in broadening the mind of the people with their assisted Tours. The Co-operative and Workers' Travel Associations have opened the way, and the chances are being taken advantage of.

Mr Yearn only works three days per week, so have to be content with making our English Guild Congress our holiday. The nearest to getting in touch with other nations is when delegates come from abroad. Then we can grip their hands in reality. Some day things will be better, and then we shall take the first opportunity. We have lived for it. If our Maker thinks otherwise we shall go to Him, believing we have tried to do our best.

We in Lancashire are thinking now a great deal of the cotton and coal industry, and are keenly dissatisfied with our present social and domestic conditions. Yet it is fine to see the grit and determination of the people to carry on, clutching at the least straw in the hope of a glimmer of the silver lining to make its appearance. I believe the Cotton Corporation is attempting to do something with its rationalisation scheme. And Mr Thomas gives some hope with his international coal orders. But we are impatiently waiting for the Government Inquiry to come along. I want if it's possible during the life of this Parliament, to show the snak of the cotton and coal owners, their inefficiency, to the general public by exposing their crude method of business.

APPENDICES

Extracts From
Guildswomen's Letters

A CHILDHOOD IN THE FENS ABOUT 1850–60

By the Late Mrs Burrows

In the very short schooling that I obtained, I learnt neither grammar nor writing. On the day that I was eight years of age, I left school, and began to work fourteen hours a day in the fields, with from forty to fifty other children of whom, even at that early age, I was the eldest. We were followed all day long by an old man carrying a long whip in his hand which he did not forget to use. A great many of the children were only five years of age. You will think that I am exaggerating, but I am *not*; it is as true as the Gospel. Thirty-five years ago is the time I speak of, and the place, Croyland in

Lincolnshire, nine miles from Peterborough. I could even now name several of the children who began at the age of five to work in the gangs, and also the name of the ganger.

We always left the town, summer and winter, the moment the old Abbey clock struck six. Anyone who has read *Hereward the Wake*, by Charles Kingsley, will have read a good description of this Abbey. We had to walk a very long way to our work, never much less than two miles each way, and very often five miles each way. The large farms all lay a good distance from the town, and it was on those farms that we worked. In the winter, by the time we reached our work, it was light enough to begin, and of course we worked until it was dark and then had our long walk home. I never remember to have reached home sooner than six and more often seven, even in winter. In the summer, we did not leave the fields in the evening until the clock had struck six, and then of course we must walk home, and this walk was no easy task for us children who had worked hard all day on the ploughed fields.

In all the four years I worked in the fields, I never worked one hour under cover of a barn, and only once did we have a meal in a house. And I shall never forget that one meal or the woman who gave us it. It was a most terrible day. The cold east wind (I suppose it was an east wind, for surely no wind ever blew colder), the sleet and snow which came every now and then in showers seemed almost to cut us to pieces. We were working upon a large farm that lay half-way between Croyland and Peterborough. Had the snow and sleet come continuously we should have been allowed to come home, but because it only came at intervals, of course we had to stay. I have been out in all sorts of weather but never remember a colder day. Well, the morning passed along somehow. The ganger did his best for us by letting us have a run in our turns, but that did not help us very much because we were too numbed with the cold to be able to run much. Dinner-time came, and we were preparing to sit down under a hedge and eat our cold dinner and drink our cold tea, when we saw the shepherd's wife coming towards us, and she said to our ganger, 'Bring these children into my house and let them eat their dinner there.' We went into that very small two-roomed cottage, and when we got into the largest room there was not standing room for us all, but this woman's heart was large, even if her house was small, and so she put her few chairs and table out into the garden, and then we all sat down in a ring upon the floor. She then placed in our midst a very large saucepan of hot boiled potatoes, and bade us help ourselves. Truly, although I have attended scores of grand parties and banquets since that time, not one of them has seemed half as good to me as that meal did. I well remember that woman. She was one of the plainest women I ever knew; in fact she was what the world would call quite ugly, and yet I can't think of her even now without thinking of that verse in one of our hymns, where it says,

'No, Earth has angels though their forms are moulded
But of such clay as fashions all below,
Though harps are wanting, and bright pinions folded,
We know them by the love-light on their brow.'

Had I time I could write how our gang of children, one winter's night, had to wade for half a mile through the flood. These floods occur nearly every winter, when the Wash overflows her banks. In harvest-time we left home at four o'clock in the morning, and stayed in the fields until it was dark, about nine o'clock. As a rule the gangs were disbanded during the harvest, each child going to work with its own friends, and when the corn was cut, the whole families would go gleaning the corn left in the fields, this being, of course, the gleaners' own property. A great many families gleaned sufficient to keep them in bread for the whole of the winter.

For four years, summer and winter, I worked in these gangs – no holidays of any sort, with the exception of very wet days and Sundays – and at the end of that time it felt like Heaven to me when I was taken to the town of Leeds, and put to work in the factory. Talk about White Slaves, the Fen districts at that time was the place to look for them.

My mother's life was one long life of loving sacrifice. It might be asked how it comes about that with such a mother, we as children should have had such a hard life of it. But the reason was not in any fault of my mother's. No woman in the world ever strove more earnestly for her children's welfare than my mother did.

My father (a well-educated and kindly-hearted man) was a great sufferer with tumour in the head. For sixteen years, he was never able to earn one day's wage, and my mother worked like a slave to keep a home over our heads. Not once to my knowledge did she ever ask or receive charity, and never did she run into debt. Scores of times I have seen her sit down to a meal of dry bread, so that we might have a tiny mite of butter on our bread, and yet she never complained. I am glad to know that in the last twenty years of her life, we were able to make her happy. When she left us one Christmas morning, we felt that never in this world should we cease to mourn for her, and no matter how long we may live, Christmas Day will nevermore be a day of unmixed pleasure to us.

As a child, I saw several opium slaves who lived in Croyland, and also several who drank large quantities of laudanum. At that time, in this town, the chemists would supply any quantity of either of these deadly drugs. I knew a child whose daily duty it was to go every morning for 1/- worth of opium, or, as it was nicknamed, 'stuff,' and very often she would have a similar quantity to fetch in the evening. A 1/- worth would be sufficient to make up into about twenty good-sized pills, and these would all be taken at one dose. Of all people on God's earth, opium slaves are the most to be pitied, for they are the most wretched. They cannot possibly live without it, and they cannot live long with it. I remember one poor old woman called Betty Rollet who cut her throat because she failed to get money to buy laudanum with it. These sort of evils, if once they take root in a town or village, soon spread.

BOOKS READ BY VARIOUS GUILDSWOMEN

Extracts from letters written in 1927

From Mrs Hood (Enfield), J.P.; a former President of the W.C.G., Poor Law Guardian, etc.

In the days before I took up Guild and other public work, I used to read a good deal, my favourite authors being Scott, Dickens and Thackeray, reading several of their works over and over again. I was also fond of poetry, Burns being my favourite; even now I steal a few moments when dusting to read some of his work. I was also fond of historical novels, in fact, history books of any kind, but alas, I find very little time for this sort of reading now. I have to keep in touch with, as much as I can, matters in connection with my public work. I read the *Daily Herald, Co-operative News, Labour Woman*, and our local weekly papers, those have to fit in at odd moments, for I do all my own housework and there is never a day scarcely that I have not to attend a meeting of some sort in connection with my work, either as a Guardian, a member of the Mosley Insurance Committee and of the local Maternity Committee, or at Labour Women's Sections and Guild Branches, besides the meetings of the Industrial Women's Standing Joint Committee.

The only time I do get for enjoyable reading is when I am on my summer holidays, and then I generally read some book that deals with the place I am visiting. For instance, when I spent my holiday in Yorkshire, I read *Wuthering Heights* and *Windyridge*, when at Gilsland in Cumberland, I read *Guy Mannering*, and when in Devonshire, I read *Lorna Doone*. Of the latest books, I have only read one of Galsworthy's, and am ashamed to say I have not read one of Hardy's, though I am longing to read *Tess*. In the meantime can you tell me of any good history of the French Revolution, not Carlyle's, please. I have tried twice to read it, and came to the conclusion you had to know all about the Revolution before you read it. In conclusion, I would say that reading would be my chief recreation if I had any time for recreation, and I only hope my eyes won't fail me when I get too old for public work, so that I will be able to indulge in my old age.

From Mrs Ferguson (Darlington), J.P., a former President of the W.C.G., Secretary of Guild Northern Section, a Director of the Darlington Co-operative Society.

I have, of course, to keep well abreast of current topics and for that I have to read the daily papers or such parts as may be of value. Then our own Co-operative press with the *Daily Herald*, and Notes for Speakers. I think these constitute the major portion of my general reading.

But I must admit that everything I can get hold of relating to International matters have a keen interest for me. I simply have to find time to dip into books which deal with International matters such as Coates on *Russia*, B. Russell on *China*, Professor Gide on *International Co-operation*, and that later book on *International Wholesales*.

I fear I have little time for the lighter side of reading, although I love a peep into Tennyson's poems, which to me are restful. My only regret is that I am unable to afford many books which I should love to possess, and I am unable at present to go often to the Library.

From Mrs Foister (Cambridge), Guild Branch and District Secretary.

I have read and much appreciated the following books during the last two and a half years:

Victor Hugo, *Les Misérables*.

Bernard Shaw, *The Doctor's Dilemma, Saint Joan*.

J. M. Barrie, *The Admirable Crichton*.

Tolstoi, *Resurrection*.

William Morris, *News from Nowhere*.

J. Dumas, *Count of Monte Cristo* (only one of series appreciated).

Hardy, *Under the Greenwood Tree*, *Far from the Madding Crowd*, *Voyages of Captain Cook*.

Dickens, *David Copperfield*, *Oliver Twist* and *Pickwick Papers*.

Charlotte Brontë, *Jane Eyre*.

George Eliot, *The Mill on the Floss*.

Jane Austen, *Pride and Prejudice*.

Blackmore, *Lorna Doone*.

Quiller Couch, *Splendid Spur*.

Sabatini, *St. Martin's Eve*.

Lytton, *Rienzi* and *Last Days of Pompeii*.

Meredith, Most and especially *The Egoist*.

Merriman, *In Kedar's Tents*.

Merekowski, *Christ and Antichrist*.

W. R. Hadwen, *Difficulties of Dr Dequesne*.

J. Haeckel, *Riddle of the Universe*.

Vachell, *Quinney's*.

Sienkiewicz, *Quo Vadis*.

Scott, *The Talisman*.

Shelley, *Selections of Poems*, especially *Adonais*.

From Mrs Axten (Cambridge),
Guild Branch Member.

The following are a few from a long list of books I have read during the last four years:

The Underworld, by James Welsh.

Children of the Dead End, by Patrick MacGill.

The Ragged Trousered Philanthropists, by Robert Tressall.

The Sowers, by Seton Merriman.

Trampling of the Lilies, by Rafael Sabatini.

The Great Hunger, by Johan Bojer.

The Rosary, by Florence Barclay.

The Veldt Trail, by Gertrude Page.

Tangled Skein and *Beau Brocade*, by Baroness Orczy.

Lena Rivers (very old book), by Mary Jane Hormes.

From Mrs Corrie (Coventry), President of Guild Branch,
Member of the Co-operative Union Central Board,
Poor Law Guardian.

I've not had much time for book reading, other than the leaflets which one must read to keep in touch with the Labour and Co-operative Movements, but I have recently re-read *Realities of War*, by Sir Philip Gibbs, to refresh my memory for dealing with the subject of Disarmament. Also *Les Misérables*, Wells' *Mr Kipps*, A.

Bennett's *Mr Prohack*, and am just going to start to read Hardy's *Tess*.

From Mrs Preston (Bury St. Edmunds),
Member of Guild Branch.

I have read a good many books, but of them all Dickens takes first place. I have rather bad nights so I always have a book by the bedside, and I find Dickens so restful. I have read *Pickwick Papers* over and over again and never tire of them.

I often wish there were more Mr Pickwicks about at the present day. I like his old-fashioned courtesy and the way he explains all his characters. I can see them so plainly that I can see some of them in everyday life.

Nicholas Nickleby is another favourite. He is such a splendid character, and the snobbery of the Ken wigs is very humorous.

I have a little boy of nine years old, and he knows *Oliver Twist* almost as well as he knows himself. *A Tale of Two Cities* I like too, and often think there were many Sydney Cartons in the Great War. Above all, I have heard Dickens was a great reformist. All honour to him!

From Mrs Burman (Bristol), Guild District Secretary.
The Happy Traveller, by Frank Tatchell, has been a veritable magic carpet to me. I particularly like his opening chapter about travelling third class. It's exactly what I should like, and very consoling.

When I made my great splash and went to Ghent, a fellow Guildswoman and myself saw a good deal of Belgium that way. Of course, if we had understood the language it would have been much better. I borrowed the book from the Public Library, so cannot give you the price, but I am hoping to get it some day; then it will rank with the map that hangs on my kitchen wall, and the old Atlas that I am afraid I study much more than my Bible.

From Mrs Woodward (Manchester), Guild Sectional Council Member.
My reading, of course, is done in time stolen from my sleeping hours, and, I am bound to confess, any meal times when alone or with my little son, who also reads whenever possible. The subjects which we Sectional Council Members have been taking, have needed much research and up-to-date information, and these I get from the newspapers and journals in the Public Library. I will

only give you a list of books which I have enjoyed, apart from lecture-preparation:

The Feminist Movement, by Mrs Philip Snowden.
Woman, by Bebel (translation).
Woman and the Church, by Maude Royden.
The Woman's Side, by Clemence Dane.
Memories and Recollections, by Lady Laura Troubridge.
Dare to be Wise, by Violet Vanbrugh.
Ten Tears After, by Sir Philip Gibbs.
Finland as it is, by De Windt.
Tribunal of the Terror, by G. Lenotre.
Her Infinite Variety, by E. V. Lucas.
One Increasing Purpose, by A. S. M. Hutchinson.
So Big, by Edna Ferber.
The Forsyte Saga, by John Galsworthy.
Tahiti, by Robert Keable.
Tell England, by Ernest Raymond.
Sorrel and Son, by Warwick Deeping.
The Amazing Interlude, by Mary Roberts.
England's Elizabeth, by Judge Parry.
The Rough Road, by W. J. Locke.
A Home and Children, by Madeline Linford.
The Hounds of Spring, by Sylvia Thompson.

All of Sheila Kaye-Smith's.
The Young Enchanted, by Hugh Walpole.
The Judge, by Rebecca West.
Crewe Train, by Rose Macaulay.
Jane, our Stranger, by Mary Borden.
Graven Image, by Margaret Widdemer.

From Mrs Rix (Bury St. Edmunds),
Guild Branch Member.

It is difficult for me to say which books I like best as so many are very fine works, and differ greatly in style and character.

Those which have interested me quite recently are a series of works entitled *Science of Thought*, by Thomas Hamblin, *Practical Psychology*, by A. Myddleton, *The Rally*, organ of International New Thought Alliance, and Works of Julia Seton Sears, M.D. In these I have found the possibility of 'Religion' being in itself a ' Science.'

Little Women and *Good Wives*, *Little Men and Jo's Boys* have been very interesting to me, and I consider that these works are those of a genius and have never been sufficiently appreciated. Dickens and Thackeray and Mrs Florence Barclay's works are favourites. I also like Shakespeare.

For poetical works, I like works of Francis Thompson – *The Hound of Heaven*, and *Poppies*. All the poems of Ella Wheeler Wilcox and those of Alice Meynell.

From Mrs Garrett (Bury St. Edmunds), Guild Branch Secretary and District Committee Member.

There is no Free Library here, which fact hampers one a good deal in reading, especially the lack of a Reference Department. Still, as ever, I read everything I come across, novels as well as poems. The following are one or two books that have helped me with my Guild Addresses:

Joseph Hyder's book on *Land Nationalisation* helps me with 'Land Problems.' Just now I am reading G. M. Trevelyan's *History of England*. This sort of book helps in many addresses, such as 'Women and Citizenship,' 'Trade Unionism,' etc.

Boots' Library has got me E. D. Simon's book on *City Council Work*, and when I have read it, I expect to gain lots of useful information to give out again in *Citizenship*.

I find that women like little speeches on biographies, and Ramsay MacDonald's book on his wife is a great favourite. I am trying to get someone to lend me a book on *Florence Nightingale*, to freshen up my memories. When we were young and ardent Socialists, my husband bound a collection of odd Socialist pamphlets in one book – Addresses by William Morris, Mrs Besant, Bernard Shaw, Hyndman, Graham Wallas and so on, and I still find them useful and inspiring.

For Peace subjects there is the mass of literature issued by the League of Nations, and I found Viscount Grey's *Autobiography* useful in 'Disarmament.' In all these things it seems that one can call up ideas and knowledge gained when one was young and was reading a great deal.

I look at our few book-shelves and at what remains after many removals about the country, and I see the names William Morris, Edward Carpenter, Tennyson, Rossetti among poets. Dickens and Scott, of course, odd volumes of Conrad, Quiller Couch, Meredith, Eden Phillpotts, Charlotte Brontë. There is Carlyle's *French Revolution* and Ruskin's *Unto this Last*. Nothing modern you see, because we haven't been buying books of late years. But I have read a fair proportion of the modern novelists, and find that in many cases the characters do not 'stay with' me. Probably because one gets older. Several of Wells' books have impressed me very much, *Tono-Bungay* and also *Men like Gods*. I found *The Disinherited Family*, by Miss Rathbone, most useful, though I strongly disagreed with the 'pools' as a remedy.

My son brought a book to me the other day (he is twenty-four). The title was *The Green Hat*, and it is by Michael Arlen. The young man wanted my opinion, which he got very forcibly. But I liked it that he asked. The strange thing is that he reads a great deal of miscellaneous stuff, but always returns to Dickens.

From Mrs White (Hampstead), Guild Branch Secretary.
After working in a Silk Mill in Leek (Staffs) till I was eighteen, I became one of the Guild Office staff. My husband, an Engineer, is a great reader, and we both have long attended the Working Men's College (Camden Town). I have read within the last two or three years:
School for John and Mary, by Elizabeth Banks. Deals with the subject of elementary education in Canada.
Life of Mary Macarthur, by Mary Hamilton.
Bygone England, by W. G. Cornish.
Men Like Gods, The Dream, Joan and Peter, by H. G. Wells.
Mr Britling Sees it Through, Saint Joan, by G. B. Shaw.
Escape, The Forsyte Saga, John Galsworthy.
Notes, by Samuel Butler.
Riceyman Steps, by Arnold Bennett.
Ariel: a Shelley Romance, by Maurois.

From Mrs Bedhall (Warwick), a former President of the
W.C.G., Poor Law Guardian.

My father was a builder, a keen educationalist and very interested in all progressive movements. He was a Pacifist, and most of us (a family of twelve) believe in Pacifist principles too. Both father and mother took a very keen interest in the literature we read. I was a teacher in an Elementary School for some years, but just prior to my marriage was a nursery governess in a private family. My husband by trade was an engineer, but owing to a very serious illness, had to leave the factory and become a chauffeur.

I get most of my books through the Students' Library belonging to the Warwickshire Education Committee. For some years I have been a member of the W.E.A. in Warwick, and this enables me to use the Library. It has been a very great help to me in getting my subject-matter together upon many of the subjects we take in the Guild Movement.

I do not get any time for novel reading, but I am fond of verse, and can get most of the good poets' works at the Library. Books I have read are:

CO-OPERATION:
Co-operative Movement in Great Britain, by B. Webb.
Co-operation in Agriculture, by H. W. Wolff.

Co-operative Banking, Principles and Practice, by H. W. Wolff.
Co-operation at Home and Abroad, by C. R. Fay.

SOCIALISM:

The Meaning of Socialism, by S. Bruce Glasier.
History of Socialism, by T. Kirkup.
Socialist Movement in England, by B. Villiers.
State Socialism in New Zealand, by S. E. Le Rossignol.
Industrial Democracy, by S. and B. Webb.

POEMS:

Leaves of Grass, by Walt Whitman.
The Minstrelsy of Peace, by S. Bruce Glasier.

TRAVEL:

English Voyages of the Sixteenth Century, by W. Raleigh.
Voyages of the Elizabethan Seamen, by R. Hakluyt.

GENERAL EDUCATIONAL BOOKS:

Democracy and Education, by J. Dewey.
The School and Society, by J. Dewey.
Education for Liberty, by K. Richmond.
The Schools and Social Reforms, by S. J. G. Hoare.
Women's Work and Wages, by E. Cadbury.

Poverty: a Study of Life, by B. Seebohm Rowntree.

Unemployment: a Social Study, by S. Rowntree and B. Tasker.

Crown of Wild Olive, Industry and War, by J. Ruskin.

Now is the Time, by A. Ponsonby.

Child Labour in the United Kingdom, by F. Keeling.

The following are some of the books I have lately been reading in connection with the Mentally Defective. I am a Guardian, and very interested in the welfare of these poor unfortunates.

Child Training, by Mrs A. H. D. Acland.

Development of the Child, by N. Oppenheim.

The State and the Child, by W. C. Hall.

Citizens Made and Re-made, by W. R. George and J. B. Stowe.

Psychology and Parenthood, by H. A. Bruce.

The Adolescent, by J. W. Slaughter.

From Mrs Bampton (Hampstead), Guild Branch Member. These are books which I found very interesting:

The Lodger, What Timmy Did, by Mrs Belloc Lowndes.
    (Both these books deal with the supernatural.)

Under the Red Rope, The Red Cockade, author not known.

These are stories of the French Revolution. I am fond of historical books.

The Village Labourer, *The Town Labourer*, by J. L. and Barbara Hammond.

The Blue Lagoon, by H. de Vere Stacpoole.

From Mrs Smith (Hampstead), Guild Branch Member.

I like *Martin Chuzzlewit*, specially for its London associations, as I am fond of books on London.

Domitia, by Baring Gould (deals with a visit to Rome).

Thoughts are Things, by Prentice Milford.

History and Power of Mind, by Richard Ingalese.

Short Stories, by Michael Arlen.

From Mrs Marshall (Cambridge), Guild Branch Member.

Hardy's *Return of the Native*.

Hardy's *Tess of the d'Urbervilles*.

Blackmore's *Lorna Doone*.

From Mrs Russell (Liverpool),
Guild Lancashire Sectional Secretary.

My time has been taken up so much with Co-operative and Guild work, and a very strenuous time in the home, that to read a book is one of the luxuries I am looking forward to with a great longing, like some do their summer holidays – but never mind it will all come in due season.

I have forgotten the titles of most of the books I have read, but not the contents. Here are some:

George Macdonald's books.

Olive Schreiner's *Dreams*, *African Farm*, etc.

Michael Fairless's *The Roadmender*.

Thomas Hardy's *Tess*, etc.

George Eliot's *Adam Bede*.

Charlotte Brontë's *Jane Eyre*, etc.

I think for amusement, *Three Men in a Boat* (author's name forgotten) is hard to beat.

Poetry I pick up at random. Fay Inchfaun is a favourite in homely poems. *Gems*, by Ella Wheeler Wilcox.

Plebs Book. *History of the British Workers*, R. W. Postgate.

All our own Co-operative literature.

The Wayside Pulpit is a source of comfort, new thoughts and education to me.

PIONEER POOR LAW GUARDIANS

From a Lincolnshire Guildswoman

I was first asked to become a candidate for the Board of Guardians previous to the property qualification being done away with, but declined. When the Act of 1894 was passed I consented to stand, and won a contested election. Twice since then, at the termination of three years' office, I have been returned without opposition.

The Vicar of the Parish opposed my nomination the first time, but on the last occasion of election, the Churchwarden sent me my nomination paper filled up, without any solicitation, showing some prejudice overcome.

The Chairman of the Board, January 1895, told the women members privately that he was much against women coming there (we were then elected but had not taken our seats), he kindly inviting us to an interview in the Board Room to make our acquaintance and explain some of our duties. He would be like the boy with the physic, he said, make the best of it. He thought we should be useful to see that the children's heads were kept clean, etc. Then he was anxious to know if we should wish to sit when speaking at the Board, as if we did, some men would too, and it was difficult enough to keep order now.

It was a great relief (so he said) when I assured him we three were accustomed to public speaking, and would not dream of addressing the Chair unless standing. (Years afterwards, when retiring, he bore generous testimony to the good work of the women, and the way in which they always *spoke to the point*.)

The interview continued: 'Where should we sit?' That chair was so and so's, and this ditto, and Mr —— would not know himself if he did not have his corner – he was sure we did not wish to inconvenience any of the *old fossils*.

I wickedly asked in my mildest manner: 'Is there anywhere that we may sit?' and a group of chairs being pointed out, I thanked him, and have now occupied one of those chairs over nine years, so probably may be esteemed one of the old 'fossils' myself. At anyrate, I am the first woman Vice-Chairman of the House Committee, and Chairman of the Nursing Committee the last three years.

Then when it was first proposed to send women to Poor Law Conferences, a cry was raised at the Board, 'Let the women stay at home and cook their husbands' dinners.' Since then for three years in succession, I have been elected as one of two representatives to the Central Poor Law Conference.

Another of our Women Guardians had worked for years at office cleaning from 5 a.m. till breakfast time, and helped to maintain her widowed mother. She has gone through the experience of being on the Guild Committee, Co-operative Education Committee, Women's Liberal Committee, Board of Guardians. She has worked in all these capacities while earning her own living.

From a Lancashire Guildswoman

When quite a young girl, not out of my teens, the Mill I worked at was burnt down. For six months I was out of work, except odd days, and during that time often knew what it was to go hungry, though no one guessed. When I resumed work I bought a penny money-box and dropped in small pieces. When full it contained nearly £4, which I placed in the Stores, and it helped me wonderfully to prepare for future rainy days.

This was all I knew of Co-operation – buying and saving – until I had the good fortune to hear of the Guild. I attended the Guild Annual Meeting, which was a revelation. Each day my vision seemed to be widening, and my spirit felt that here was the very opportunity I had always been seeking but never put into words. I had longings and aspirations and a vague idea of power within myself which had never had an opportunity of realisation. At the close of the Meetings I felt as I imagine a War Horse must feel when he hears the beat of the drums.

I formerly held the view that my husband could manage my politics – that there was no need for me to have a vote. I heard the question debated at an Annual Meeting, read, and thought the matter out, and came to the conclusion that a human responsibility cannot be taken by another. Each, whether man or woman, must use their own responsibility.

It was a long step to go from such a narrow view of women's duties to believing that women ought not only to vote but to take part in the administration of the Law so far as they were allowed, and hoping for still greater privileges, I not only believed in this but was willing to brave opposition and fight for a seat. Men bitterly resented this advent of women in their special preserves. This has been lived down, and expressions such as 'I do not know what we should do without our Women Guardians' have been often heard. They have also been made Chairmen of important administrative Committees.

Honours, such as opening new buildings, have been conferred upon them – a great victory over prejudice against women. One of our Poor Law Guardians is rather deaf. In describing his difficulty in following the business, through this defect, he said: 'I watch the women and vote as they do, and I was never far wrong.' This is all the greater compliment from the fact that he holds political views opposite to our own.

At a Ward meeting called to choose candidates, an Alderman said he was in favour of putting another woman in, for he was convinced in his own mind that they made the best Guardians.

It is rather a puzzle to myself when I look back, how I have managed to make all my public duties fit in with my home duties. In the first place I have had a splendid constitution, and the busy life seems to have suited me. Most of my lectures and addresses have been thought out when my hands have been busy in household duties – in the wash-tub, when baking (and by the way I have never bought a week's baking during my married life of over twenty-one years), or doing out my rooms. Somehow the time passes more quickly, and I have not felt the work so hard when my mind has been filled with other things. I have always been very methodical in the house. Monday, washing and ironing. Tuesday for tidying up my rooms and sewing, and preparing a dinner for Wednesday, my Poor Law day. Thursday, I bake and do my bedrooms. Friday, with the help of a charwoman for half-day, I go through the rest of the house. Every other Saturday, two or three hours for Poor Law, odds and ends of sewing, and providing for the weekend. I never change this programme, except in case of sickness. Guild work and Poor Law work sometimes clash, but as most of my meetings are within easy distance they do not interfere much with home, as I invariably do my work before I go, and I always try to have my nights free, either to take a meeting or read at home.

It would be impossible to tell you of the scheming there is to be done to keep things comfortable. I have the reputation in Yorkshire as 'that woman who gets up in the middle of the night to go home.' This is because I always try to leave early if it is convenient to my hostess, hurrying home to have a good hot dinner (thanks to my gas stove); other times when they have had a cold dinner I try to get something nice and hot for tea.

If one had not a real love for the work, the task is too hard. I have ridden in all kinds of vehicles, including bread carts, to outside country places. I have once gone from here to Grimsby and back in the day. I have also gone to London and back, and taken a meeting, in twenty hours. I have trudged through the snow and rain with my bag, and I have carried my bag in my hand until my fingers have tingled with the frost, feeling that I should have been better at home. All this has been changed when I have met with a cheery reception, and I have looked down upon the earnest eager faces of Co-operative friends. On the whole the gain has been mine, for my experiences in persons, places, and modes of life in other Counties have been a veritable education.

My house is our own, but if we rented it we should have to pay about 12/6 per week. The one we lived in during our early married life was 5/- per week. In those days I made 18/6 per week, and kept the house going after my rent was deducted. I had my family quickly, and my dividend helped me over these times, and paid the doctor's bill. In fact I do not know how I could have managed without it, as I have always been determined to keep free from debt.

PIT-HEAD BATHS

From a Mid-Lancashire Guildswoman

My husband has been employed at a colliery where there are baths at the pit-head for the past fifteen years, as fireman, and he was one of the first to make use of the baths. He has also washed himself at the baths for the above period of years without being afflicted with any cold or rheumatism or illness. He thinks that it is a great improvement for the workers, because, going to and fro from the colliery, they always have a change of fresh clothes when it is raining, from wet clothes to dry ones. He says:

'As an official, we finish winding at 2.45 p.m. I go straight to the lamp-room and gives my lamp in, and after goes to the baths which are only about forty yards away. I take off all my pit clothes and goes into the bath, and washes all dirt and dust from my body from head to foot. After I am washed I comes into the room and put on all my clean clothes, collar and tie, etc., and altogether it take about twenty minutes to wash and change, and get on your way home. The men does not mind the delay in getting home, as long as they are washed and clean. If you saw the workers coming home after they have washed and changed, you would not think that they worked at the pit – collar and tie and clean clothes. After you are washed you feel made over again. At our pit, the workers does not pay anything at all.

'We never have our clothes washed or mended at the colliery. When the clothing is done with, they (the miners) take them home and bring on a fresh suit because, when a worker has used his clothes underground for six or eight months and they get ragged, he brings them home, either for to be mended or for a fresh suit.

'The miners and officials at our colliery who are washing themselves at the baths are about 90 per cent, so you see they are all in favour of baths. We bring our own towels and soap, and we always bring our clothes home every week to be washed, with the exception of our trousers, jacket and waistcoat and clogs. All the above arrangements cannot be improved as I think they are O.K.

'The baths are a building improvised for so many men. They are also heated with pipes, say three inch or four inch hot water pipes, to go round the building, cubicles, baths, one person in each bath at a time. Two sets of one inch pipes are arranged in each bath, and also two valves, one for hot water and another for cold, according to temperature, and also a one inch pipe comes through from hot and cold to an overhead spray for washing all dirt from the workers. The place where the pit clothes are kept dry is arranged in the same building where the worker washes himself. The arrangement is to have a fixture all round the building so that he can wind his own clothes up with a rope (cotton) about halfway up the building, according to the hot water pipes which you have arranged previous.'

About making less dirt and work in the home, I think it is a great improvement for the housewife. The majority of the miners' wives whose husbands work at the colliery, would think that there was something wrong if she saw her husband in a black face.

The majority of the workers' wives don't know what it is to have dirty bedding-clothes, and also dirt or dust lying about the house. I think that it is far better to have baths at the collieries than have them in the houses. Reason why? The housewife has not the dust or dirt to contend with when her husband washes himself at the pit baths, and in the other case she has all the dirt and the dust to contend with, and also all the pit clothes lying about the house, causing dust to raise and get all over everything, causing more dusting and cleaning for the wife.

From a Durham Guildswoman

The pit-head baths have been established here since 1926, and the cost to my husband in 3d. per week, which is deducted from his wages by the company. Soap and towel can be bought at cost price at the baths, and are supplied by the C.W.S. The cubicles in which the men wash are the overhead spray type. Washing is much pleasanter under this system than the old bathtub method, the cold spray making the men less susceptible to colds and pains. Also the regulated heat of the baths and the shorter time taken in having a bath (ten minutes is the limit in the cubicles) are advantageous.

My home life has been greatly improved by the inception of the baths, a cleanliness which is very noticeable as compared with the time prior to the building of the baths. The dirt of the mine is reduced to an absolute minimum, for the pit clothes are left at the baths, as are the pit boots which are cleaned and greased in the boot-room there. Electric brushes clean the boots and the oil is applied by a hand brush. The absence of the pit clothes creates a sweeter atmosphere in the home, for the clothes carry with them a smell peculiar to mine-working, and when the pit clothes are present, the house is permeated with this peculiar smell. Clothing is kept much cleaner, especially underwear, for the grime of the mine is much more effectively cleansed away by the pit-head baths than it was by the old-fashioned bath-tub.

More attention can be paid by the housewife in preparing the table for meals for the workers after coming home from the baths. A clean cloth can be used, and when the meal is taken, no evidence of mine-work is present. Having no pit clothes to deal with does away with a tremendous amount of dirty work, especially when there are two or three miners in the home. Water had to be boiled for washing purposes, and at the same time, dinner had to be cooked on the one fire. Pit boots had to be greased, pit clothes had to be shook and put away only to be brought out at night for the shift next day. The tidiness of the home was subject to the times of the various shifts. Thus the home never had that look of cleanliness and contentment that now exists. As to whether I should prefer bathrooms in the home or the pithead baths, I would most certainly advocate the former, as not only would my husband receive the benefit as at present, but the entire family would benefit.

A MEMBER'S VIEW OF THE GUILD

From a London Guildswoman

I can hardly gauge what the Guild has done for me. I feel it has affected me in so many different ways. There were certain latent sparks which it has kindled and caused to burn brightly. It has given me a much greater under-standing of life and an immense feeling of sympathy with men and women in general. How our lives are linked together and each may work for a common good, though we may never see or speak to one another. I feel more and more what an immense power united action can be, and how the humblest may attain to it in its best form. I think that is one of the best features in the Guild. Though I feel diffident, and know my ignorance, it has given me courage to speak boldly even at Men's Meetings outside the Co-operative Movement. Any influence I may have had I feel is due entirely to the Guild. The one great dif-ference between the Guild and other bodies of women I have come in contact with, is, may I say, its splendid Democracy. The humblest member can feel that she stands on an absolute equality with the most lofty. Also there is a feeling of comradeship absent in the same degree in other associations. I have heard other women say practically the same thing, and say how it has taught them to think on social questions they at one time would have passed over as outside their capacity. I have seen women join and have seen this change take place. They have certainly become less self-centred and more public-spirited. In words which our members often use, 'it has brought us out.'

AFTERWORD
by Anna Davin and Gloden Dallas

Personal testimony, like the memoirs here reprinted, has a particular importance for anyone who is interested in the history of ordinary people, and most of all for those who want to explore hidden areas like the experience of childhood and family and the lives of women. There is plenty of material for other kinds of history – archives full of the records of government and law, of trade and transport, of every kind of institution. These can tell us something about working class life, but the perspective is that of administration not experience; it is information collected by outsiders and coloured by their assumptions and beliefs. Clergymen, teachers, doctors, employers, charity workers, and anyone else who could claim a nodding acquaintance with the poor gave evidence to countless official and unofficial investigations of working class life and labour;

and the same people often left letters and autobiographies recording their impressions (sometimes vivid, sometimes stereotyped and facetious) of 'how the poor lived'.

Working class witnesses were few; and their evidence was defined by the interests of the investigators, and limited too no doubt by class barriers and often the formal context of the enquiry – too like a court. They were never children and rarely women. Working class memoirs and autobiographies, too, are comparatively few, and by women are rarer still.

So *Life As We Have Known It* has exceptional value as providing accounts by 'us' rather than 'them', and as dealing not just with the generalities of working class life, but with the specific experience of women, as they chose to tell them. They recount here their lives as children, as workers, as housewives slaving and skimping and contriving; and also, perhaps most movingly, they describe their struggles for intellectual and political self-development. Again and again they convey the excitement of learning with the support and encouragement of other women Co-operators to speak out and act as individuals, to represent their branches of the Women's Co-operative Guild or the Guild itself, even to take on wider responsibilities in local government. The Guild taught them 'what an immense power united action can be, and how the humblest may attain to it in its best form'; it gave them confidence to think and stand up for themselves, to fight for maternity benefits, divorce, education, insurance and, of course, the vote: it 'brought them out', as they said themselves. How right that their accounts should have been published and preserved through the Guild's long-serving General Secretary, Margaret Llewelyn Davies.

Virginia Woolf's connection with the Guild is surprising enough to need comment. There is a deep feminism in her literary work, and a sympathy for women striving for themselves and others; she believed in the need for suffrage and equality for women; but she had little active interest (or faith) in organized politics. (In 1910 however after a conversation with her old suffragist friend and teacher Janet Case she decided, uncharacteristically, 'that action is necessary', and joined the Adult Suffrage League, in which her efforts amounted to 'writing names like Cowgill on envelopes'.) The coincidence of her marriage to Leonard Woolf, an active Fabian, and her friendship with Margaret Llewelyn Davies (who 'could compel a steam roller to waltz') brought her close to the strongly pro-suffrage Guild, and in June 1913 she attended their conference in Newcastle. Seventeen years later, in the introductory letter reprinted here, she described her sense of separation from the assembled women, 'the contradictory and complex feelings which beset the middle class visitor when forced to sit through a Congress of women in silence'. She approved their demands, yet 'if every reform they demand was granted this very instant it would not touch one hair of my comfortable capitalistic head'. Moreover their enthusiasm seemed useless since not one of them had the vote, without which there could be no change.

At the congress she felt 'irretrievably cut off from the actors', and thereafter her links with the Guild, though maintained, were sporadic, often interrupted by severe mental breakdowns – one, for instance, only six weeks after the Newcastle meeting. During her recovery in 1914 she wrote, 'By occupying myself with typewriting and Co-operative manuals I keep cheerful . . . '; and from 1916 she ran the Richmond branch of the Guild. Perhaps this closer experience of ordinary members and routine work resolved some of the uncertainties she had felt in Newcastle. Certainly letters sent by Guildswomen to Margaret Llewelyn Davies which Virginia Woolf read during those years moved her to a closer appreciation of their lives, and of the value of their organization. In 1914 she was urging the publication of *Letters on Maternity*, preferably in full and with lots of photographs. By 1930 in the introductory letter, she still admits her dilemma as a middle class woman, but also shows greater under-standing, affection and respect for those women who had so puzzled her in 1913. This ambivalence, her sense of being 'the benevolent spectator', stayed with her all her life, but of all political organizations only the Guild seems to have touched her heart. In 1916 she wrote to Margaret Llewelyn Davies,

> But then, my dear Miss Davies, what does do good? You may be sitting on Town Councils and upholding one's ideals. I incline to think that merely improves one's own soul – still I dare say the Women's Guild has done some-thing; isn't it touching how I return to that achievement of yours always for comfort?

ANNA DAVIN and GLODEN DALLAS, 1977

Anna Davin is a social historian researching childhood, family and women's work in nineteenth century London and a founding editor of *History Workshop Journal*.

Gloden Dallas was a social historian, the co-author of *The Unknown Army: Mutinies in the British Army in World War 1* (Verso, 1985), with Douglas Gill. A mother of three, she studied and supported the women's movement throughout her life.

NOTE ON THE WOMEN'S
CO-OPERATIVE GUILD

By the Editor

Besides being primarily a record of individual experiences, the Memories of Co-operative Women bring out the part that is played by the workers' own Movements in their everyday life. These Movements are very different from philanthropic and social reform organizations. Trade Unionism and Co-operation are woven into the very fabric of the workers' lives. Trade Unionists stretch the warp of a decent living wage. Co-operators thread the woof of intelligent spending on their own manufactured goods, thus gaining control of industry by the people for the people.

So little is generally known of Consumers' Co-operation that the numerous allusions to it in the preceeding pages require a brief explanation of the Movement.

People are apt to think of Co-operation as a thrift

movement, or to associate it with the Army and Navy Stores. How little is it realised by economists and others that Co-operation is the beginning of a great revolution! The Movement shows in practice that there is nothing visionary or impossible in the aspirations of those who desire to see the Community in control, instead of the Capitalists. Under the Co-operative system, no individuals can make fortunes, Co-operators evidently believing, like the old writer, that 'money is like muck, no good unless it is spread.' No 'profits' are made; the surplus, inseparable from trading, is shared among the purchasers, according to the amount each spends. Capital becomes the tool of labour, and not its master.

Men and women, as members of their local Co-operative Societies, own the shops where they buy, supply their own capital (on which a fixed interest is paid), and manage their business through elected committees and members' meetings, where the rule of one man one vote prevails. Federated together, over 1,000 Societies with some 6,000,000 members constitute the English and Scottish Co-operative Wholesale Societies. These, combined, form one of the largest trading and manufacturing concerns in Great Britain. The local

Societies are also federated into the Co-operative Union for educational, legal and propagandist purposes, and, through the Co-operative Party, are allied politically with the Labour Party. The Movement also takes an active part in the International Co-operative Alliance, to which thirty-four countries are affiliated.

This peaceful revolution from autocratic Capitalism to democratic Co-operation is based on the women's Marketing Basket. Isolated in their own individual homes, it is through their common everyday interests as buyers that married working-women have come together, and found their place in the labour world and national life. The Women's Co-operative Guild,* with nearly 1,400 branches and 67,000 members, has given the unity and force which enable the women to become a power in the Movement and to share in its administration. Each Branch of the Guild manages its own affairs, and Branches are associated in self-governing Districts and Sections. For the whole Guild a Central Committee is elected, and a Congress, attended by 1,000 delegates and presided over by the working-woman President for the year, crowns the year's work.

* The Guild was founded by Mrs Acland and Mrs Lawrenson in 1883.

It is usual to regard education as quite apart from practice. But the characteristic of the Guild education is that it is bound up with appropriate action. This combination is naturally attractive to practical housewives. The study of Co-operation leads Guild women not only to buy consistently at the Store, but also to press forward enlightened policies affecting the whole Movement.

There has been, and still is, the usual struggle to obtain 'Seats for Women', but many Guild members are on the Management and Educational Committees of their Societies, several are on the Co-operative Union, and one has been elected as a Director of the Co-operative Wholesale Society. A recent article in the *Co-operative News* has described the Guild as 'a living link between leaders and the rank and file . . . It joins the Co-operative factory to the Co-operative home and makes Co-operation the vital issue at thousands of firesides . . . It is a power-house of Co-operative ideas and initiative as well as a testing house for Co-operative policy . . . The Guild lives and grows because it refuses to wait till opportunity knocks at the door. It makes opportunity, then uses it vigorously to promote its own and the Co-operation's cause.'

Outside the Co-operative Movement, Guildswomen have effectively voiced the neglected needs of married working-women. They supported vigorously the establishment of School Clinics. They brought forward a National Scheme for the care of Maternity, which included many of the points now advocated by the Ministry of Health. After working for the inclusion of Maternity Benefit in the Insurance Act, the Guild was successful in securing Maternity Benefit as the property of the wife. The Guild has also made a notable contribution to breaking down class and sex disabilities in public life. Ten Guildswomen are Aldermen, eighty-one are on County and Municipal Councils, eighty-three are magistrates, and many more are taking part in the varied work of numerous public committees.

It will be seen in the Memories that Guildswomen, starting from buying bread and butter on revolutionary principles, have reached an international outlook. This has led to the creation of an International Co-operative Women's Guild, in which twenty-seven countries, including Soviet Russia, are now taking part. At its recent Congress (1930) in Vienna, attended by over 250 delegates from twenty countries, discussions took place on the legal co-operative status of women, and whether the economic position of women should be best solved by State family allowances or factory work. A previous subject had been 'The Family Wash,' and methods from riverside washing to co-operative washhouses with electrical labour-saving appliances were illustrated by photographs taken, not only in European countries, but in Japan.

The international Guild has steadfastly stood for Peace, and has laid before the League of Nations the strong demand of its members for Disarmament.

Margaret Llewelyn Davies

1931

NO ONE BUT A WOMAN KNOWS
Stories of Motherhood Before the War

Edited by Margaret Llewelyn Davies

'I was married at twenty and a mother of three by twenty-three . . . When I look back at the first three years of my marriage, I wonder how I lived through it.'

When it was published in 1915 this book provoked a sensation – for the first time, working women were able to put across their view of maternity. These humbling autobiographical portraits are as valuable today as they were almost a hundred years ago: in their own words these women tell of the horrors of bringing ten children into the world in as many years; of not being able to afford a doctor or nurse; of the physical and emotional strain of bringing up large families with very little help.

These extraordinary and inspiring stories of poverty and hardship remind us of the astounding endurance of women and of the strength of a mother's love.